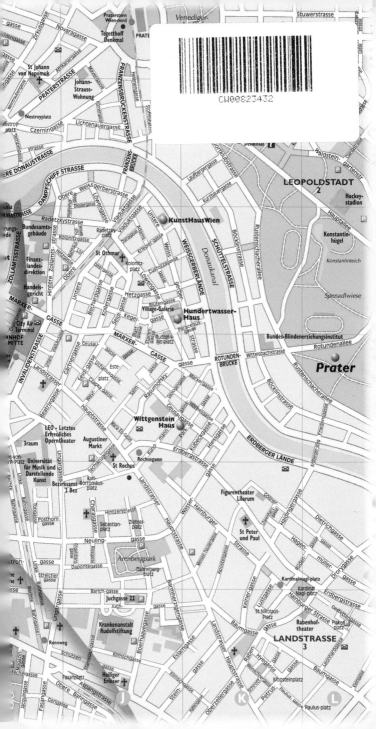

AA

CITYPACK
Vienna

How to Use This Book

KEY TO SYMBOLS

✚	Map reference to the accompanying fold-out map	🚢	Nearest riverboat or ferry stop
✉	Address	♿	Facilities for visitors with disabilities
☎	Telephone number	❓	Other practical information
🕐	Opening/closing times	▷	Further information
🍴	Restaurant or café	ℹ	Tourist information
🚆	Nearest rail station	✋	Admission charges: Expensive (over €10), Moderate (€5–€10) and Inexpensive (less than €5)
Ⓜ	Nearest Metro (subway) station		
🚌	Nearest bus route		

This guide is divided into four sections

● Essential Vienna: An introduction to the city and tips on making the most of your stay.

● Vienna by Area: We've broken the city into five areas, and recommended the best sights, shops, entertainment venues, nightlife and restaurants in each one. Suggested walks help you to explore on foot.

● Where to Stay: The best hotels, whether you're looking for luxury, budget or something in between.

● Need to Know: The info you need to make your trip run smoothly, including getting about by public transportation, weather tips, emergency phone numbers and useful websites.

Navigation In the Vienna by Area chapter, we've given each area its own color, which is also used on the locator maps throughout the book and the map on the inside front cover.

Maps The fold-out map with this book is a comprehensive street plan of Vienna. The grid on this fold-out map is the same as the grid on the locator maps within the book. We've given grid references within the book for each sight and listing.

Contents

ESSENTIAL VIENNA   **4–18**

Introducing Vienna   4–5
A Short Stay in Vienna   6–7
Top 25   8–9
Shopping   10–11
Shopping by Theme   12
Vienna by Night   13
Where to Eat   14
Where to Eat by Cuisine   15
Top Tips For...   16–18

VIENNA BY AREA   **19–106**
INNERE STADT   **20–46**

Area Map   22–23
Sights   24–35
Walk   36–37
Shopping   38–40
Entertainment
    and Nightlife   41–42
Where to Eat   43–46

RINGSTRASSE   **47–64**

Area Map   48–49
Sights   50–58
Walk   59
Shopping   60
Entertainment
    and Nightlife   61
Where to Eat   62–64

AROUND ALSERGRUND   **65–76**

Area Map   66–67
Sights   68–71
Walk   72
Shopping   73
Entertainment
    and Nightlife   74
Where to Eat   75–76

**AROUND LANDSTRASSE,
WIEDEN**   **77–90**

Area Map   78–79
Sights   80–85
Walk   86
Shopping   87
Entertainment
    and Nightlife   88
Where to Eat   89–90

FARTHER AFIELD   **91–106**

Area Map   92–93
Sights   94–101
Excursions   102–104
Shopping   105
Entertainment
    and Nightlife   105
Where to Eat   106

WHERE TO STAY   **107–112**

Introduction   108
Budget Hotels   109
Mid-Range Hotels   110–111
Luxury Hotels   112

NEED TO KNOW   **113–125**

Planning Ahead   114–115
Getting There   116–117
Getting Around   118–119
Essential Facts   120–121
Language   122–123
Timeline   124–125

CONTENTS

Introducing Vienna

Set in the heart of Central Europe, Vienna has always attracted visitors for its imperial treasures and outstanding cultural heritage. However, it has also gained a reputation for being at the forefront of the European fashion, art and food scenes.

The cosmopolitan metropolis of Vienna is not typical of Austria as a whole. It is rather an icon of the rich past of Central Europe; but at the same time it is ultramodern, an economic hot spot, as its businesses take advantage of successful European integration and seize new opportunities for investment and growth.

The Rathausplatz has become particularly lively. People gather here for ice-skating in winter, for the Social Democrats' 1 May parade and for the spectacular opening of the Vienna Arts Festival shortly afterward. There are open-air showings of music and opera films every evening in July and August, and from mid-November to Christmas Eve the glittering *Christkindlmarkt* is a major family attraction. It is also from here that the *Silvesterpfad* (New Year's Eve Walk) starts its meandering route

toward Stephansplatz, where the Cathedral's great bell rings in the New Year while the crowds dance to the Blue Danube Waltz.

The Hofburg is another focal point of the city. In the Imperial Treasury you come face to face with the history of Central Europe, Habsburg power and the symbolic relics of Empire; if treasures are not your thing, you can see a musical performance at the Spanish Riding School; or, if you're prepared to rise early on a Sunday, go along to a sung Mass performed by the Vienna Boys' Choir in the Burgkapelle. But the "Burg" is not only a monument to the past: History is still being made here. Politicians, diplomats, officials and scientists from all over the world have been assembling in the Hofburg since Vienna became the third official seat of the United Nations.

FACTS AND FIGURES

● The population of Vienna is 1.73 million. The non-Austrian population of Vienna stands at almost 20 percent.

● Over 50,000 of the 185,000 pre-World War II Jewish-Viennese population died in the Holocaust.

● The metropolitan area has around 2.6 million inhabitants, meaning that one in five Austrians live in or near the capital city.

VIENNESE DIALECT

Viennese dialect is sophisticated and has a long tradition on stage and in cabaret, even in verse. Vivid and lively, but impenetrable to outsiders, it is both a vibrant assertion of identity and a means whereby the Viennese can shelter their own private sphere in a city full of tourists and new arrivals. Naturally most can switch to accented standard German when required.

LOCAL CONSERVATISM

The Viennese exhibit very strong local patriotism, coupled with a certain conservatism that ensures each new architectural project is greeted with cries of righteous scorn. However it seems things have always been this way: The critics complained of the Opera on its completion in 1869 that it looked like an "elephant lying down to digest its dinner."

MUST BE TIME FOR A MEAL

An astonishing 4,000 eateries cater to the Viennese need for meals at all times of the day. Extracurricular consumption includes at least one "coffee-pause" in the morning, and maybe a *Jause* (a hefty snack of bread, charcuterie and cheese) to stave off hunger pangs between serious eating. The locals cheerfully joke about "suicide by knife and fork".

A Short Stay in Vienna

DAY 1

Morning Start at the Opera (U-Bahn and tram stops). Just behind it is the famous **Hotel Sacher** (▷ 112) where you can enjoy a coffee and a slice of Sachertorte in the hotel's coffeehouse. From here head to the nearby **Kaisergruft** (Capuchin Crypt, ▷ 29) on the Neuer Markt to view the tombs of the Habsburg emperors.

Mid-morning Next to the Neuer Markt is Kärntner Strasse, from which you approach **Stephansdom** (St. Stephen's Cathedral, ▷ 31), the spiritual and topographical heart of the city. From the deeply sacred, move abruptly to the very secular: In a narrow backstreet behind the cathedral is the **Mozarthaus** (▷ 34) where the composer wrote his most satirical work, *The Marriage of Figaro*.

Lunch Enjoy a meal in the intimate garden of the **Haas & Haas** teahouse (▷ 39), accessed from the southwest corner of the cathedral square (Stephansplatz).

Afternoon From Stephansplatz walk north along the Graben, then turn left down the Kohlmarkt. Ahead of you is the vast complex of the **Hofburg** (▷ 26), the former Imperial Palace of the Habsburgs. Cross the Ringstrasse via the Heldentor to the **Kunsthistorisches Museum** (▷ 52) with its superb collection of pictures and applied art.

Dinner Across the River Wien a fine-dining experience awaits you at **Steirereck** (▷ 89), one of Vienna's finest restaurants.

Evening Close the day with a walk along the Ringstrasse to view the great Historicist architecture of the 19th century, beautifully illuminated at night.

DAY 2

Morning Start the day with breakfast in **Café Schwarzenberg** (▷ 62) opposite the **Hotel Imperial** (▷ 112) on the Ringstrasse. From there it is a short walk to the **Hochstrahlbrunnen** (▷ 85), a 19th-century fountain, and the huge Russian War Memorial behind it, both at the southern end of **Schwarzenbergplatz**. Then bear left and follow the Rennweg to the main entrance of **Schloss Belvedere** (▷ 82).

Mid-morning The highlight of the Lower Belvedere is the Golden Salon (*cabinet doré*) and Balthasar Permoser's statue (1721) of Prince Eugene of Savoy, whose palace this was. Climb the hill through the park to the Upper Belvedere with its splendid collection of paintings, including works by Klimt, Schiele and Kokoschka.

Lunch Salm Bräu (▷ 89) is a great place for midday meal—try the traditional Viennese dish of *Tafelspitz* (boiled beef and a dish you must try on your trip) followed by delicious apricot strudel served with vanilla ice cream.

Afternoon For a complete change of theme and scene, take U1 (U-Bahn) from Südtirolerplatz-Hauptbahnhof to Praterstern. In the **Prater** (▷ 98) you can take a ride on the Ferris wheel or one of the many other attractions before going back to Schwedenplatz with U1. From here it is a short walk to the **Jewish Quarter** (▷ 28) and Judenplatz.

Dinner Indulge in some people-watching in the glassed terrace of one of Vienna's top Italian restaurants, **Fabios** (▷ 44).

Evening Take in an opera performance in the **Staatsoper** (▷ 35) or a concert in the gilded auditorium of the **Musikverein** (▷ 88).

Top 25

TOP
25

▶ ▶ ▶

Akademie der Bildenden Künste ▷ 50 World-renowned gallery with five centuries of art.

Burgtheater ▷ 51 This theater has a staircase partly decorated by the young Klimt and his brother.

Coffeehouses ▷ 24 The soul of Vienna can be found in a coffee cup and topped by whipped cream.

Wien Museum ▷ 84 One of Europe's best city museums tells the history of the city from the Celts onward.

Stephansdom ▷ 31 Masterpieces of late Gothic sculpture and baroque altarpieces in this cathedral.

Secession ▷ 56 Landmark building of the Vienna Secession, housing Gustav Klimt's *Beethoven Frieze*.

Schloss Schönbrunn ▷ 99 Summer palace of the Habsburgs with fine gardens and a zoo.

Schloss Belvedere ▷ 82–83 Baroque gardens and two palaces, both housing a core collection of Austrian art.

Rathaus ▷ 55 The neo-Gothic City Hall is the administrative heart of the city and has frequent events on the square in front of it.

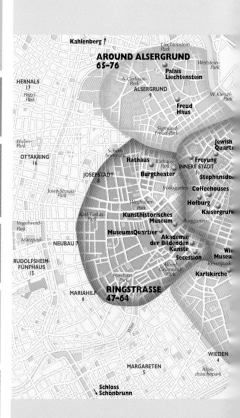

Prater and Riesenrad ▷ 98 Amusement park and the Ferris wheel featured in *The Third Man*.

Palais Liechtenstein ▷ 70 A palace housing the Liechtenstein family's art collection.

MuTh ▷ 97 Hear the world's best-known boys' choir in their permanent new home.

These pages are a quick guide to the Top 25, which are described in more detail later. Here they are listed alphabetically, and the tinted background shows which area they are in.

Danube Cruise ▷ 94
Cruises within Vienna and downstream to the Slovak capital, Bratislava.

Freud Haus ▷ 68–69
The home of the founder of psychoanalysis until his emigration in 1938.

Freyung ▷ 25 Baroque palaces and the monastery which gave the square its name.

Heeresgeschichtliches Museum ▷ 80 A military-history museum in a vast complex.

Hofburg ▷ 26–27 The former Imperial Palace was the Habsburg dynasty's residence for six centuries.

Hundertwasser-Haus and KunstHausWien ▷ 95 Postmodern follies designed by Friedensreich Hundertwasser.

Jewish Quarter ▷ 28 One of Vienna's oldest and most historic quarters, centered on Judenplatz.

Kahlenburg ▷ 96 A spur of the Wienerwald with fine views over the city.

Kaisergruft ▷ 29 Richly ornate coffins in the Imperial Crypt.

Karlskirche ▷ 81 St. Charles's Church is a masterwork of Fischer von Erlach, father and son.

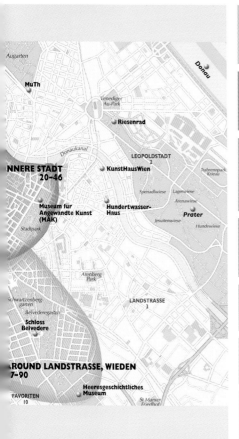

MuseumsQuartier ▷ 54 Exciting district with several museums and interactive spaces.

Museum für Angewandte Kunst (MAK) ▷ 30 Vienna's Museum of Applied Art.

Kunsthistorisches Museum ▷ 52–53 Famous works by Brueghel and Rubens.

◀ ◀ ◀

Shopping

Vienna offers a diverse mix of shopping. International main-street names and outlets of famous designers are easily discovered but the real treasures can be found in modern boutiques selling the dynamic and the quirky, and in the independent stores stocking the quaint and charming.

Souvenirs and Gifts

Tracht (traditional costume) is found in shops all over the city. If you don't want to go the whole hog of *Dirndlkleid* or *Lederhosen*, look for the more restrained *Steirer-Jacke* (Styrian jacket with decorative edgings) or the wonderfully enduring Loden overcoats, or even a smart Austrian hat.

Austrians are good at designing charming ornaments, some of which admittedly border on kitsch. Typical are the models of animals and birds made in a variety of different materials. Decorative enamel influenced by the Wiener Werkstätte, the leading producer of which is Michaela Frey, is also attractive, while purses and handbags embroidered with petit point also make nice presents. Porcelain comes from two great names: Augarten in Vienna and the Gmundner Keramik from Upper Austria. The latter, with its green motifs, is a folksy affair, while the Augarten is formal and aristocratic.

Local Delicacies

Vienna has plenty of local delicacies—ideal if you are looking for edible gifts to take home.

SHOPPING AREAS

Shopping in the city can roughly be divided into luxury, middle market and cheap. The area comprising Kohlmarkt, Graben and Kärntner Strasse offers chic Austrian goods and international designer labels. Mariahilferstrasse is Vienna's Oxford Street, with the last of the big stores (good for household items and clothing). Cheapest of all is the flea market *(Flohmarkt)* at the west end of the Naschmarkt each Saturday morning—packed with bargains or fun for browsing.

Clockwise from top: Christmas shopping; Christmas market; clothing boutique; shopping mall; antiques-hunting

The famous Sachertorte (a chocolate cake invented in 1832) can be shipped anywhere for you from the Sacher shop, likewise the rival *Imperialtorte*. Then there are the Mozart Kugel (gold-wrapped spherical chocolates filled with marzipan and nougat) and the Mozart Thaler (the same, but shaped like coins). These are the trademark Austrian chocolates, but many other *chocolatiers* produce goodies just as good. Austrian wine remains slightly under-rated (the whites, like Grüner Veltliner or Riesling from the Wachau, are recommended) and the *Sekt* is better than its reputation as the poor man's champagne. *Obstler* (schnapps made from various fruits) is an Austrian specialty much prized by those in the know.

Traditional Music

Nothing gives a better taste of a country than its music. A huge selection of CDs of Austrian music (including one-off performances such as the traditional New Year's Eve and New Year concerts of the Vienna Philharmonic at the Musikverein) is on sale in the city. Works by Johann Strauss (the Waltz King) are ubiquitous, as are the indigenous art forms of operetta (Lehár, Kálmán) and *Schrammel* music from the *Heurigen* (taverns). Austrian Broadcasting (ORF) has produced a comprehensive anthology of *Wiener Lieder*. Music to accompany performances of the Spanish Riding School can be obtained on CD.

MOVING WITH THE TIMES

There was a time when Viennese shopkeepers called all the shots, but much has changed. Despite opposition from retailers, shopping hours have been greatly improved: No longer do sad crowds mill around the windows of closed shops on Saturday afternoon; no more do book-store assistants crouch over the tills, glaring suspiciously at browsers. And for those who want to shop till they drop, there are now several constantly expanding shopping malls. The biggest is the aptly named Shopping City Süd. An alternative is the Ringstrassen Galerien.

Shopping by Theme

Whether you're looking for a department store, a quirky boutique, or something in between, you'll find it in Vienna. On this page, shops are listed by theme. For a more detailed write-up, see the individual listings in Vienna by Area.

Accessories
Alois Frimmel (▷ 87)
Derby-Handschuhe
    (▷ 38)
Ina Kent Wien (▷ 60)
Köchert (▷ 39)
Mühlbauer (▷ 39)
Robert Horn (▷ 40)
Szászi Hüte (▷ 60)

Antiques and Art
Dorotheum (▷ 38)
Galerie Heike Curtze
    (▷ 38)
Galerie Wolfrum (▷ 38)
Hundertwasser Village
    (▷ 105)
WOKA (▷ 40)

**Books, Maps
  and Music**
Doblinger (▷ 38)
Frick am Graben (▷ 38)
Shakespeare & Company
    (▷ 40)

Clothing and Shoes
Flo Vintage (▷ 87)
Knize (▷ 39)
Mariol (▷ 87)
Tostmann Trachten
    (▷ 73)

Food and Wine
Altmann & Kühne (▷ 38)
Demmers Teehaus
    (▷ 73)
Haas & Haas (▷ 39)
Julius Meinl am Graben
    (▷ 39)
Manner Factory Outlet
    (▷ 105)
Metzger (▷ 39)
Pischinger (▷ 87)
Unger und Klein (▷ 73)
Xocolat Manufaktur
    (▷ 73)

Glass and China
Augarten (▷ 38)
J. & L. Lobmeyr (▷ 39)
Österreichische
    Werkstätten (▷ 40)
Wiener Porzellanfabrik
    (▷ 105)

Jewelry
Köchert (▷ 39)
Rauminhalt (▷ 60)
Wiener Interieur (▷ 40)

Markets
Christkindlmarkt (▷ 60)
Naschmarkt (▷ 60)
Neubaugasse (▷ 60)
Spittelberg Market
    (▷ 60)

**Shopping Malls and
  Department Stores**
BahnhofCity (▷ 87)
Ringstrassen-Galerien
    (▷ 60)
Steffl (▷ 40)

Toys
Edi-Bär (▷ 87)
Fürnis Mädchen und
    Buben (▷ 73)
Pinocchio (▷ 40)

Vienna by Night

New *Szenelokale* (fashionable or "in" bars and restaurants) open every year in Vienna. These are concentrated in certain areas—the best known is the so-called Bermuda Dreieck (Bermuda Triangle) to the west of Schwedenplatz.

Where to Go

The Spittelberg area is a good example of inner- city revival with its effortlessly chic and charming venues. Here you can sit in an 18th-century courtyard, or on a street flanked by baroque and Biedermeier facades, enjoying a wide range of cuisines, or check out the many bars and Italian-style cafés. A fun nighttime atmosphere has developed in the area from Stephansdom to Am Hof and between Josefstädterstrasse and Laudongasse in the Josefstadt, a region frequented by intellectuals and the well-to-do.

Wine Taverns

An entire culture revolves around the wine taverns of Vienna's peripheral villages, Grinzing, Heiligenstadt, Salmannsdorf and Neustift am Walde being the best known. You may prefer this to the bustle of the city; here you can sip white wine in the peace of a *Heuriger* (▷ 106) garden and tuck into a *Heuriger* buffet.

Floodlit Monuments

Perhaps the greatest evening pleasure is entirely free, namely walking around the floodlit monuments of the Inner City.

From top: Rathaus at dusk; the Blumenrad, in the Prater; Karlskirche illuminated at night

BALMY EVENINGS

Exploiting five and a half months of mild to warm weather, in Vienna you can linger at café or restaurant tables on the sidewalk outside, or in *Heurigen* gardens, until late into the evening. A restaurant extension is known as a *Schanigarten*, from the nickname of the first person to erect one on the Graben in 1754. In summer there are also major open-air events, among them the jazz festival on the Donauinsel and the opera films in front of the Rathaus.

Where to Eat

The general standard of Viennese cuisine is high, even at the cheaper end of the market. The Nordsee chain offers very acceptable fast-food fish dishes and there is a broad range of middle-price *gute bürgerliche Küche* cuisine. But gourmets will not go hungry either.

World Influences

Vienna's kitchen has always been a mixture of Austrian recipes and those of its Central European neighbors, formerly part of the Habsburg Empire. The famous Wiener schnitzel is derived from the *scaloppina Milanese* from Lombardy, goulash was imported from Hungary, and some Bohemian dishes (chiefly various kinds of dumplings) have survived here. Over the past decade, an invasion of the Turkish doner kebab has followed the pizza wave, although this is more a feature of the suburbs than the main tourist areas.

Run the Gamut from Beef to Ice Cream

Austria is a land-locked country and Vienna's cooking has always focused on meat and cereals. Beef (especially boiled beef, called *Tafelspitz*) has a long tradition in the city; in the few restaurants that concentrate on it, the variety of beef dishes is amazing. Everything depends upon the quality of the beef itself, as well as careful preparation and fresh condiments, if the real *Tafelspitz* experience is to be enjoyed. Moving from the savory to the sweet, Vienna's ice-cream parlors have a selection and quality to rival those of Italy and are the ideal post-dinner treat.

THAT UNIQUE LOCAL EXPERIENCE

Specific to Vienna are the *Heurigen* (wine taverns) on the outskirts of the city. In the old town of the inner city, there are also deep wine cellars, sometimes descending two levels through baroque to Gothic foundations. Above ground in summer, you can lunch in one of the popular garden restaurants or dine in a princely palace.

Viennese cakes and pastries— especially the famous Sachertorte—can be enjoyed in the city's coffeehouses

Where to Eat by Cuisine

There are places to eat to suit all tastes and budgets in Vienna. On this page they are listed by cuisine. For a more detailed description of each venue, see Vienna by Area.

Beisl
Beim Czaak (▷ 43)
Glacis Beisl
 (panel, ▷ 54, 62)
Kern's Beisl (▷ 45)
Restaurant Wiener
 (▷ 63)

Cellars
Esterhazykeller (▷ 44)
Piaristenkeller (▷ 62)
Rathauskeller (▷ 63)
Salm Bräu (▷ 89)

Coffeehouses and Cafés
Aida (▷ 43)
Berg (▷ 75)
Café Bräunerhof (▷ 24)
Café Central (▷ 43)
Café Diglas (▷ 43)
Café Drechsler (▷ 62)
Café Eiles (▷ 62)
Café am Heumarkt
 (▷ 89)
Café Landtmann (▷ 62)
Café Leopold Hawelka
 (▷ 24)
Café Prückel (▷ 44)
Café Sacher (▷ 44)
Café Schwarzenberg
 (▷ 62)
Café Sperl (▷ 62)
Demel (▷ 44)
Dommayer (▷ 106)
Heiner (▷ 45)

Heurigen
Fuhrgassl-Huber (▷ 106)
Mayer am Pfarrplatz
 (▷ 106)

International
Do & Co (▷ 44)
Ethiopian Restaurant
 (▷ 75)
Restaurant Lale (▷ 45)

Italian
Casa Alberto (▷ 89)
Fabios (▷ 44)

Seafood
Kornat (▷ 45)
Ragusa (▷ 75)

Vegetarian
Wrenkh (▷ 45)

Vienna's Best
Badeschiff (▷ 45)
Bristol Lounge (▷ 43)
Donauturm (▷ 106)
Plachutta (▷ 45, 106)
Das Schick (▷ 63)
Sluka (▷ 63)
Steirereck (▷ 89)

Viennese/Austrian
Figlmüller (▷ 44)
Klein Steiermark (▷ 89)
Meinl am Graben (▷ 45)
Porzellan (▷ 75)
Rochusmarkt (▷ 89)
Roth (▷ 75)
Servitenwirt (▷ 75)
Wild (▷ 106)
Zu ebener Erde und
 erster Stock (▷ 63)

Top Tips For...

These suggestions will help you tailor your ideal visit to Vienna, no matter how you choose to spend your time. Each sight or listing has a fuller write-up elsewhere in the book.

CLASSICAL MUSIC
Practice your conducting in the Haus der Musik (▷ 33).
Savor the musicianship of the Wiener Philharmoniker in the Golden Hall of the Musikverein (▷ 88).
Pay homage to Mozart at the Mozarthaus (▷ 34), where he once lodged.

COFFEEHOUSES
Order the original Sachertorte at Café Sacher (▷ 44), in the celebrated Hotel Sacher—or have it mailed to friends (or yourself) from the Sacher shop.
Meet friends at Café Landtmann (▷ 62).
Indulge yourself at Demel patisserie (▷ 44), a former purveyor to the imperial household.

ANTIQUES SHOPPING
Buy Augarten porcelain (▷ 38) decorated with floral designs in the former Augarten Palace, now a factory for this famous ware.
Bid at an auction at "Aunt Dorothy" (Dorotheum, ▷ 38), Vienna's traditional auction house.

CLOTHES AND ACCESSORIES
Have a gentleman's suit made for you at Knize's shop (▷ 39).
Splash out on a luxurious handbag at Ina Kent Wien (▷ 60).
Check out the headgear at Szászi Hüte—a hat for every occasion (▷ 60).
Have one of Austria's signature felt hats made to measure at Mühlbauer (▷ 39).
Look the part with a traditional folk outfit from the long-established supplier Tostmann Trachten (▷ 73).

Clockwise from top left: Musikverein; The Ankeruhr; Hotel Imperial; Eat or drink in a Viennese cellar or Beisl;

WHAT'S FREE

Enjoy music films on a huge screen in front of the Rathaus (July and August, ▷ 55).
Walk to or from the Kahlenberg through woods and vineyards (▷ 96).
Watch the figures of the Ankeruhr move across the clockface at noon (▷ 28).

HOTELS WITH CHARACTER

Enjoy a cutting-edge hotel experience at the slick Do & Co (▷ 112).
Indulge your love of wine at the unique Hotel Rathaus Wine and Design (▷ 111).
Combine Viennese tradition with modern comfort at Hotel Sacher (▷ 112).
Mingle with kings and presidents at Hotel Imperial (▷ 112), which is used as official accommodations for state visitors.

ATMOSPHERIC RESTAURANTS

Enjoy the food in the cavernous interior of the Rathaus at the Rathauskeller (▷ 63).
Soak in the atmosphere of the Austro-Hungarian monarchy in the Piaristenkeller (▷ 62).
Eat in a traditional Beisl, such as Beim Czaak (▷ 43).

NIGHTLIFE

Join an evening roof walk of St. Stephen's Cathedral (▷ 31).
Meet Vienna's high society at the exclusive Eden Bar (▷ 41).
Dance through the night with local and international DJs at Flex, beside the Danube Canal (▷ 61).
Get your feet tapping to Austrian and international jazz acts at Porgy & Bess (▷ 42).
Kick back by the Danube at Vienna's first beach club Strandbar Herrmann (▷ 42).
Check out the lastest European flicks at Burgkino (▷ 61).
Add a splash of creativity to your city break at Europe's most happening arts venue, Wuk (▷ 74).

St. Stephen's Cathedral after dark; Shop for that perfect hat or antiques; cakes galore in Vienna's coffeehouses

AUSTRIAN SECESSION AND EXPRESSIONISTS

Be sure to see the "Golden Cabbage" on top of the Secession (▷ 56)—and the *Beethoven Frieze* in the Secession basement.

Don't miss the paintings by Klimt, Schiele and Kokoschka at the gallery in the Upper Belvedere (▷ 82).

Look inside Otto Wagner's Postsparkassenamt (▷ 34) for its dazzling white hall.

Join a guided tour of Wagner's Kirche am Steinhof (▷ 100), which combines functionalism with beauty.

CHILDREN'S ACTIVITIES

Ride the Ferris wheel and try some of the other attractions in the Prater (▷ 98).

Take a boat tour of the Seegrotte in Hinterbrühl (▷ 104), Europe's largest underground lake.

Get lost in the baroque labyrinth of the park at Schloss Schönbrunn (▷ 99); children can also enjoy the zoo.

Keep boredom at bay in the MuseumsQuartier with a puppet or dance performance at Dschungel Wien (▷ 61).

Watch eyes light up as the little'uns peruse the offerings of the traditional toyshop Pinocchio (▷ 40).

SHOE-STRING ACCOMMODATIONS

Arrive home at the Time Out City Hotel (▷ 109) to enjoy family-style comfort in Jugendstil opulence.

Save money by staying in one of the city's many private rooms (▷ 109).

LUXURY LIVING

Do a spot of jewelry shopping at exclusive Köchert (▷ 39), though you'll need a fat wallet to afford anything.

Try the gourmet version of Tafelspitz at the luxury restaurant Plachutta (▷ 45).

Dine in the glassed terrace of Fabios, Vienna's authentic Italian eatery (▷ 44).

From top: The Secession; riding the Ferris wheel in the Prater; stay in comfort during your visit; relaxing with wine

Vienna by Area

Innere Stadt 20–46

Ringstrasse 47–64

Around Alsergrund 65–76

Around Landstrasse, Wieden 77–90

Farther Afield 91–106

Innere Stadt

St. Stephen's Cathedral and the imperial palace of the Hofburg are the highlights of Vienna's ancient and historic heart, but everywhere in the Innere Stadt you will encounter the entire palette of architectural styles and curiosities.

Top 25

Coffeehouses	**24**
Freyung	**25**
Hofburg	**26**
Jewish Quarter	**28**
Kaisergruft	**29**
Museum für Angewandte Kunst (MAK)	**30**
Stephansdom	**31**
More to See	32
Walk	**36**
Shopping	**38**
Entertainment and Nightlife	**41**
Where to Eat	**43**

2

3

4

5

6

FRANZ-JOSEFS-KAI

Donaukanal

Börse

Börsegasse

Wipplingerstrasse

Börse
platz

Conzatta gasse

Essling gasse

Franz-Josef-Kai

Neutorgasse

Werdertorgasse

Heinrichsgasse

Rudolfs
platz

Gölsdorfgasse

Schottenbastei

Schottengasse

Hohenstaufengasse

Helferstorfer

Salzgries

Concordia-
platz

Marc-Aurel-Strasse

Salztorgasse

Molker
Bastei

Schottenstift

Schottenkirche

Renngasse

Tiefer

Graben

Feuerwehr-
museum

Salvatorgasse

Maria am
Gestade

Wipplingerstrasse

Altes
Rathaus

Pasqualatihaus

Schreyvogelgasse

Oppolzer

Freyung

Judenplatz

Teinfalt-strasse

Löwelstrasse

Kunstforum

Holocaust
Memorial

Jewish
Quarter

Hoher
Markt

INNERE STADT

Am Hof

Uhrenmuseum

Bognergasse

Tuchlauben

Schenken
strasse

Bank
gasse

Herrengasse

Naglergasse

Peterskirche

Brand-
stätte

Kramergasse

Esperanto
Museum

Wallnerstrasse

Bauern

cold-schmiedgasse

Dom- u
Diözesan-mus

Minoriten-
kirche

Herrengasse

Globenmuseum

Kohlmarkt

Artaria
Haus

Pestsäule

Graben

Haas-
Haus

Stephansdo

Minoritenplatz

Loos
Haus

St
Michael

Bundeskanzler-
amt

Schauflergasse

Michaeler-
platz

Habsburgergasse

Stephansplatz

Stephansplatz

Sin

Ballhaus-
platz

Alte Hofburg

Reitschulgasse

Dorotheergasse

Bräunerstrasse

Coffeehouses

Stock-i-
Eisen-Platz

Schatzkammer

Seilergasse

Neuer
Markt

Weihb

Sisi Museum

Hofburg

Spiegelgasse

Donner
Brunnen

Kärntner-
strasse

Prinz-Eugen-
Denkmal

National-
bibliothek

Augustiner-
kirche

Augustinerstrasse

Kaisergruft

Himmelp
gasse

Neue
Burg

Lobkowitz-
Palais

Annakirche

Burgtor
(Heldentor)

Albertina

Führich

Tegetthoffstrasse

Maltese
Kirche

Annagasse

Johan

Seile

Burggarten

Theatermus Gedenkr
Staatsopernmus

Albertina
Platz

Haus der
Musik

Schwarzenberg

Waifischgasse

Stadt Theater

OPERNRING

Staatsoper

Mahler-
strasse

strasse

OPERNGASSE

Kärntnerstrasse

KÄRNTNER RING

Oper

Bösen-

dorferstrasse

Akademie

strasse

Canova

Karlsplatz

Kunstlerhaus

Dumba

Otto Wagner
Pavillon

Neuer
Markt

Mustk-
verein

Resselpark
Karlsplatz

0   250 m
0   250 yds

D   **E**   **F**

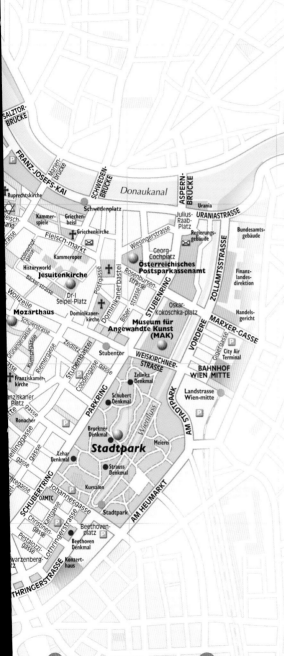

SALZTOR-BRÜCKE

FRANZ-JOSEFS-KAI

Marienbrücke

SCHWEDENBRÜCKE

Donaukanal

ASPERNBRÜCKE

Ruprechtskirche

Fleisch-markt

Schwedenplatz

Urania

Julius-Raab-Platz

URANIASTRASSE

ZOLLAMTSSTRASSE

Bundesamtsgebäude

Kammerspiele

Griechenbeisl

Fleisch-markt

Griechenkirche

Wiesingerstrasse

Regierungsgebäude

Finanzlandesdirektion

Kühnergasse

Kammeroper

Georg-Cochplatz

Österreichisches Postsparkassenamt

Historyworld

Jesuitenkirche

Rosenbursenstrasse

Bäckerstrasse

STUBENRING

Oskar-Kokoschka-platz

Handelsgericht

Wollzeile

Dr-I Seipel-Platz

Dominikanerbastei

Biber-strasse

Postgasse

Mozarthaus

Dominikanerkirche

Museum für Angewandte Kunst (MAK)

VORDERE

MARXER-GASSE

Schulerstrasse

Zedlitzgasse

City Air Terminal

Grünangergasse

Riemergasse

Stubenbastei

Stubentor

Coburggasse

WEISKIRCHNERSTRASSE

Clarragasse

BAHNHOF WIEN MITTE

Franziskanerkirche

Franziskaner Platz

PARKRING

Zelinka Denkmal

AM STADTPARK

Landstrasse Wien-mitte

Weihburggasse

Schubert Denkmal

Ronacher

Seilerstätte

Bruckner Denkmal

Stadtpark

Wienfluss

Meierei

Annagasse

Lehar Denkmal

Strauss Denkmal

SCHUBERTRING

Johannesgasse

Kursalon

AM HEUMARKT

OAMTC

Christinengasse

Stadtpark

Lothringerstrasse

Canovagasse

Beethovenplatz

Pestalozzigasse

Beethoven Denkmal

Schwarzenbergplatz

Konzerthaus

RINGSTRASSE

G

H

Coffeehouses

TOP 25

Linger in a coffeehouse and enjoy the atmosphere as well as the coffee and cakes

THE BASICS

Café Bräunerhof
braeunerhof.at
F4
Stallburggasse 2
512 38 93
Mon–Sat 8–6, Sun 10–6
U1, U3 to Stephansdom
Moderate

Café Leopold Hawelka
hawelka.at
F4
Dorotheergasse 6
512 82 30
Mon–Sat 8am–midnight, Sun 10am–midnight
U1, U3 to Stephansdom
Inexpensive

TIP

- Coffeehouses serve more than just coffee. You can almost always get beer or wine, decent traditional Austrian food, and, of course, ice cream and cakes. They also have newspapers and magazines for their customers' use.

Coffeehouses are an integral part of Vienna's culture. They function as public living rooms or lounges; places to meet friends, grab a meal or quick bite, or merely take a solitary coffee break.

History Legend has it that coffee first came to Vienna via the Turks during their siege of the city in the late 17th century. By the 19th century, the Wiener Kaffeehaus—with its trademark *grand salons* and stuffy waiters—was firmly entrenched on the local scene. The list of *stammgäste* (regulars) to Vienna's coffeehouses over the years reads like a Who's Who of European luminaries—from Vladimir Lenin to Sigmund Freud.

Protocol Coffeehouses are usually relaxed affairs, but it helps to know a few rules. The first concerns which coffee to order. The four most common ones are: *Kleiner schwarzer* (small black coffee, similar to espresso); *Kleiner brauner* (espresso with a shot of milk); *Verlängerter* (means "stretched" in German, hot water added to espresso like an Americano); and *Melange* (a *Verlängerter* with foamed milk, like a cappuccino).

Where to find them Just about every neighborhood in the city has a classic coffeehouse, but most tend to be in the Innere Stadt and around the Ringstrasse. Two popular ones in the Innere Stadt are Café Bräunerhof and Café Leopold Hawelka.

This irregularly shaped square is hemmed with fascinating buildings that can easily take up a couple of hours of your time in the city. It's one of Vienna's prettiest locations and ideal for wandering.

Freyung This square acquired its name (meaning "asylum") due to the adjacent Benedictine monastery, which until 1848 had the right to give asylum to fugitives from justice.

Schottenkirche The Abbey Church of the "Schotten" Benedictines, dominating the east side of the square, was called Scottish because the Latin name for Ireland was *Scotia maior*. The 15th-century Gothic altarpiece, now in the Museum im Schottenstift in the Schottenkirche, shows the earliest existing view of Vienna.

Palais Ferstel This structure is not actually a palace but a complex named after its architect. Inside, a glass-roofed arcade lined with gift shops leads from the Freyung to Herrengasse ("Street of the Lords"). It was formerly the seat of the Vienna Stock Exchange.

Kinsky-Palais This is one of Lukas von Hildebrandt's masterworks and was built in 1716, with a slim, elegant facade that overlooks the Freyung. Try to get a look at the ceremonial staircase inside and also its ceiling fresco, *Apotheosis of a War Hero*, which flatters Count Philipp von Daun, the military commander who first owned the palace.

THE BASICS

schottenstift.at

+ E3

✉ Schottenkirche and Museum im Schottenstift: Freyung 6. Palais Ferstel: Freyung 2

☎ Schottenkirche: 534 98 200. Museum: 534 98 600

🕙 Schottenkirche: usually daily 7am–9pm. Museum: Thu–Fri 11–5, Sat 11–4.30

🍴 Café Central in Palais Ferstel (▷ 43)

🚇 U2 to Schottentor, U3 to Herrengasse

🚹 Few

💲 Inexpensive

HIGHLIGHTS

Freyung
● Medieval cobbles in the northeast corner
● Hildebrandt's Kinsky-Palais, Freyung 4
Schottenkirche and Schottenstift Museum
● Gothic wing altar, Master of the Scots 1469–80
● High altar (Ferstel)
● Tomb of Count Starhemberg
Palais Ferstel
● Danube Fountain

Hofburg

HIGHLIGHTS

● Imperial Treasury
● Imperial Apartments
with Silver Collection
● Court Chapel and Vienna
Boys' Choir
● Spanish Riding School
● Prunksaal of the
National Library

TIP

● After a trip to the
Spanish Riding School,
continue the equestrian
theme by picking up a
horse-drawn carriage
in Heldenplatz.

**It is said that the Habsburgs never
finished their great projects; the Hofburg
(the former imperial residence), like
St. Stephen's Cathedral (▷ 31) and the
Habsburg Empire itself, is an example of
their unfinished business.**

Traditions In terms of history, the Hofburg (the
Habsburg residence) is more significant than all
other buildings in Vienna. The Schatzkammer
houses secular and sacred treasuries, including
the crowns of the Holy Roman Empire and of
the Empire of Austria. Three institutions still
operate in the Hofburg: the Hofmusikkapelle
(Court Music Chapel), where the Wiener
Sängerknaben (Vienna Boys' Choir) sing
Sunday Mass in the Burgkapelle (Court Chapel;
mid-Sep to Jun); the Spanische Hofreitschule

Dripping in luxury, the Hofburg impresses both inside and out

THE BASICS

hofburg-wien.at
hofmusikkapelle.gv.at
srs.at

🔢 E5

✉ Imperial Apartments, Sisi Museum, Silver and Tableware Collection: Hofburg—Michaelerkuppel; Nationalbibliothek: Josefplatz 1; Burgkapelle: Hofburg—Schweizerhof

☎ Imperial Apartments, Sisi Museum, Silver and Tableware Collection: 533 75 70; Nationalbibliothek: 534 100; Burgkapelle: 533 99 27

🕐 Imperial Apartments, Sisi Museum, Silver and Tableware Collection: Daily 9–5.30 (Jul–Aug 9–6). Guided tours daily 2pm; Treasury: Wed–Mon 10–6; Burgkapelle: Mass mid-Sep to Jun Sun 9.15, reservation needed; Riding School: morning training (with music) daily 10–noon, performances Sat–Sun 11 (tickets from visitor center at Michaelerplatz 1), summer and winter break guided tours daily 2, 3 and 4 (reservations tel: 533 90 31); Prunksaal of the National Library: Tue–Sun 10–6, Thu 10–9

🚇 U3 to Herrengasse

🚌 Bus 2A, 3A to Hofburg

♿ Few; good for library

💶 Expensive

(Spanish Riding School), a center of equestrian excellence famed for its dancing horses; and the Nationalbibliothek (National Library).

Architecture The earliest fortress here was built in 1275 on the site that became the Schweizerhof (Swiss Court), named after the former Swiss Guard. The Schweizerhof incorporates the Gothic Burgkapelle and the Renaissance Schweizertor (Swiss Gate). There were baroque extensions of the original Hofburg. The Neue Hofburg, partially framing the Heldenplatz (Heroes Square) was built in Historicist style and completed on the eve of World War I. On the square are the equestrian statues of Prince Eugene of Savoy (hero of the Turkish Wars) and Archduke Charles (victor of the Battle of Aspern against Napoleon).

INNERE STADT TOP 25
</>

Jewish Quarter

TOP 25

The Ankeruhr on Hoher Markt (left); the Holocaust Memorial on Judenplatz (right)

THE BASICS

⊹ F3

Stadttempel

jmw.at

✉ Seitenstettengasse 4

☎ 535 04 31 33

🕐 By guided tour only: Mon–Thu 11.30, 2

🚇 U1, U4 to Schwedenplatz

🚌 Bus 3A to Hoher Markt; tram 1 to Schwedenplatz

♿ Excellent

✋ Inexpensive

Jüdisches Museum Wien

jmw.at

✉ Misrachi Haus, Judenplatz 8

☎ 535 04 31

🕐 Sun–Thu 10–6, Fri 10–5

🚇 U1, U3 to Stephansplatz

🚌 Bus 3A to Hoher Markt

♿ Excellent

✋ Inexpensive

Jüdisches Museum Wien/Dorotheergasse

✉ Dorotheergasse 11

☎ 535 04 31

🕐 Sun–Fri 10–6

🚇 U1, U3 to Stephansplatz

♿ Excellent

✋ Inexpensive

Vienna's historic Jewish Quarter has two focal points: the old Stadttempel and the modern Holocaust Memorial. Today's Jewish community is northeast of the Danube Canal.

Stadttempel Hidden behind a simple facade, the neoclassical synagogue in Seitenstetten-gasse is the only place of Jewish worship that survived the Nazi atrocities in Vienna. The offices of the Jewish community and other institutions are in the building.

Hoher Markt and Altes Rathaus En route from Judengasse to Judenplatz you cross Hoher Markt. At its northeast corner is the famous Ankeruhr (Franz von Matsch, 1913). Every hour a different figure from Austrian history revolves around the clock face, while at noon all the figures appear in sequence. The former City Hall (Altes Rathaus) in Wipplingerstrasse is overshadowed by the mighty facade of the former Bohemian Court Chancellery across the street.

Holocaust Memorial Judenplatz was the heart of the medieval ghetto. Remains of a synagogue can be seen beneath the Jewish Museum at Misrachi Haus, while the square is dominated by Rachel Whiteread's Holocaust Memorial, which remembers the 65,000 Austrian Jews killed in World War II. A branch of the Jewish Museum, on Dorotheergasse, focuses on contemporary Jewish life in Vienna.

28
</>

Imperial tombs (left);
a macabre detail of
Karl VI's tomb in the
Capuchin Crypt (right)

Deceased emperors' hearts are preserved in the Augustinian Church (▷ 32), their embalmed entrails in St. Stephen's (▷ 31) and their bodies here in the Capuchin Crypt, a shrine for pilgrims and loyalists.

The Capuchins and their church The Franciscan Capuchins came to Austria in the reign of Duke (later Emperor) Matthias (1612–19), whose wife, Empress Anna, founded their monastery in 1618. The preacher Marco d'Aviano was Vienna's most celebrated Capuchin. Famously intrepid, he went into battle with the imperial forces against the Turkish, which was besieging Vienna in 1683. He is buried in one of the church's chapels.

Simplicity The building is a perfect reflection of the austere principles of the Capuchins. Almost the only decoration is a 1936 fresco of St. Francis of Assisi and a cross on the facade. Inside is the Kaiserkapelle (Emperor Chapel), with wooden statues of emperors Matthias and Ferdinand II, III and IV. The Chapel of the Cross has an altar by Lukas von Hildebrandt and a moving pietà (Mary embracing the dead Christ).

Habsburg resting place The first emperor and empress to be buried in the crypt were Matthias and his wife Anna. Since then 138 members of the Habsburg family have been interred here, along with Maria Theresa's governess. The simple copper coffin of Joseph II is a reminder of its occupant's distaste for religious excess.

THE BASICS

kaisergruft.at
🟦 F5
✉ Tegetthoffstrasse 2
☎ 512 685 316
🕐 Daily 10–6
🚇 U1, U3 to Stephansplatz
🚌 Bus 3A to Albertinaplatz
♿ Good
🎟 Church free; crypt inexpensive

HIGHLIGHTS

The church
● Bronze of Marco d'Aviano
● Statues of four emperors
● Marble altar by Hildebrandt
● Pietà, by Peter Strudel and Matthias Steinl
The crypt
● Tomb of Charles IV
● Double tomb of Franz Stephan and Maria Theresa
● Tombs of Franz Joseph and Elisabeth
● Bust of the last emperor, Karl, and coffin of the last empress, Zita

Museum für Angewandte Kunst (MAK)

Chair by Josef Hoffmann; (left) museum interior (middle); Wiener Werkstätte vase (right)

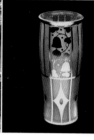

THE BASICS

mak.at
� H4
✉ Stubenring 5
☎ 711 360; recorded information 711 36 248
🕐 Tue 10–10, Wed–Sun 10–6
🍴 Elegant café
🚆 S-Bahn to Landstrasse
🚇 U3 to Stubentor, U4 to Landstrasse-Wien Mitte
🚋 Tram 2 to Stubentor
♿ Good
💶 Moderate; free admission Sat
❓ Guided tours in English Sun at noon. Frequent special exhibitions

HIGHLIGHTS

● Atrium
● 16th-century Egyptian silk carpet
● 15th-century Buddha head
● Meissen bear
● Bohemian glass
● Lobmeyr glass (Vienna)

MAK isn't your usual applied arts and craft museum. It explores the union of applied art, design, contemporary art and architecture through striking displays and exhibits.

Forerunner Established in 1864, the MAK was the first museum of its kind in Europe. The initiative came from art historian Rudolf Eitelberger, who had been much impressed by London's South Kensington Museum, later the Victoria and Albert Museum.

Decorative The 1871 neo-Renaissance building by Heinrich Ferstel combines architecture with applied art—its facade is ornamented with sgraffito and majolica portrait medallions of artist-craftsmen. The entrance leads to a beautiful atrium, with arcades around each floor. In contrast, a glass-and-steel passageway connects different parts of the building.

The collections A striking example of minimalist display techniques used by MAK is the projection of silhouettes of chairs against a white screen, which emphasizes the beauty of the designs. But this is just one example of the rich collections the museum has, which also includes a fine selection featuring the work of Werkstätte, Jugendstil, Biedermeier and Thonet. There is a section devoted to objects from the East, and another part contains European decorative art, including Venetian and Bohemian glass, Meissen porcelain, and jewelry.

Stephansdom

Elaborately carved pulpit in the cathedral (left); the striking tiled roof (right)

St. Stephen's Cathedral has been the spiritual focus of the Viennese people since the Middle Ages—its massive Pummerin Bell rings in the New Year. The great South Tower is affectionately known as the Steffl ("Little Steve").

Admire the exterior From the three earlier Romanesque churches on this site, only the Giant's Door and Heathen Towers (so called because a pagan shrine was supposed to have been here) have survived as part of the Gothic church. Note the striking yellow, green and black chevrons of the tiled roof and a representation of the Habsburg double-headed eagle. Against the north external wall is the pulpit marking the spot where Giovanni Capistrano (1386–1456) preached fiery sermons against the Turks. The cathedral is considered a symbol of endurance, having undergone numerous repairs due to the ravages of the Turks, the Napoleonic French and the Allies. All the Federal States contributed to the cathedral's restoration after World War II.

Inside Anton Pilgram's late Gothic pulpit with portraits of the fathers of the church is near the entrance. Above the organ loft of the north aisle is a sculpted self-portrait of Pilgram holding a square and compass. The Gothic vaulting in the Albertine Choir is especially beautiful. Tobias Pock's 1647 baroque altar painting shows the martyrdom of St. Stephen. In the south apse is the marble tomb of Friedrich III.

THE BASICS

stephanskirche.at

🔁 F4

✉ Stephansplatz 3

☎ 51 552 30 54

🕐 Church, catacombs, treasury and bell tower: Mon–Sat 9–11.30, 1–4.30; Sun 1–4.30. South tower: Daily 9–5.30

🚇 U1, U3 to Stephansplatz

🚌 Buses 1A, 2A

♿ Main church: good

💶 Church: free; choir: moderate (guided tour only); catacombs, bell tower, treasury, south tower: inexpensive; combined ticket: expensive

❓ Evening tours in English Jun–Sep Sat 7pm (meet at south tower reception, moderate)

HIGHLIGHTS

● Pilgram's pulpit
● Tomb of Prince Eugene of Savoy, Kreuzkapelle
● Pummerin Bell
● Nicolas van Leyden's tomb of Friedrich III (1440–93)

More to See

ALBERTINA

albertina.at

Louis Montoyer built this gallery between 1801 and 1804 to house the magnificent collection of artworks assembled by Duke Albert of Sachsen-Teschen. The Albertina is the world's leading graphic collection, comprising more than a million items. Its famous drawings and etchings are kept in controlled conditions to preserve them and are seldom on display, because light would damage their delicate and fragile structure.

🔢 F5 ✉ Albertinaplatz 1 ☎ 534 830 🕐 Daily 9–6, Wed & Fri 9–9 🚇 U1, U2, U4 to Karlsplatz, U3 to Stephansplatz 🚌 Bus 3A to Albertinaplatz 🚻 Good 💰 Moderate ❓ Tours: audio guide in English

ANNAKIRCHE

annakirche.at

An intimate gem of early 17th-century baroque architecture, with Daniel Gran's ceiling fresco of the Immaculate Conception. In the side chapel is a beautiful Gothic carving of Mary, Jesus and St. Anne by Veit Stoss of Nürnberg.

🔢 F5 ✉ Annagasse 3B ☎ 512 47 97 🕐 Daily 9–12, 2.30–5.30 🚇 U1, U3 to Stephansplatz

ARTARIA HAUS

Max Fabiani's Artaria House is one of the most striking Jugendstil buildings in the city. It's an example of the early Jugendstil style with unusual bay windows and marble cladding. It's now offices with a shop on the ground floor.

🔢 F4 ✉ Kohlmarkt 9 🚇 U3 to Herrengasse

AUGUSTINERKIRCHE

augustinerkirche.at

The Church of St. Augustine, the parish church of the Habsburg court, can seem forbidding from the exterior. In its Loreto Chapel are preserved the hearts of members of the imperial family. On Sunday Vienna's best-sung Masses cheer things up.

🔢 F5 ✉ Augustinerstrasse 3 (entrance Josefsplatz) 🕐 Mon–Sat 7.30–7.30, Sun 1–6, sung Mass Sep–Jun Sun 11 🚇 U1, U2, U4 to Karlsplatz/Oper, U3 to Herrengasse 🚌 Hopper 3A to Albertinaplatz 🚻 Church only 💰 Inexpensive ❓ Tour of Loreto Chapel and Herzgruft after Mass Sun

BURGGARTEN

The vast Jugendstil glasshouse, built by Friedrich Ohmann in 1907, now houses a restaurant and bars; the terrace is a great spot in Summer.

🔢 E5 ✉ Opernring 🕐 Mar–Oct daily 10am–2am; Nov–Feb Mon–Thu 11.30am–midnight, Fri–Sat 10am–1am, Sun 10am–midnight. Closed Mon–Tue in Jan–Feb 🚋 Trams 1, 2, D to Burgring

The baroque Annakirche

DONNER BRUNNEN

This is a copy of Georg Raphael Donner's Providentia Fountain, which stands in the Belvedere (▷ 82–83). Sovereign Maria Theresa disapproved of the nude figures. The water nymphs symbolize the rivers of Lower Austria.

🔢 F5 ✉ Neuer Markt 🚇 U1, U3 to Stephansplatz

ESPERANTO MUSEUM

onb.ac.at

A unique collection featuring invented languages. It covers everything from philosophical considerations to terminology, the planning of new languages and intervention in existing ones.

🔢 E4 ✉ Palais Mollard ☎ 534 10 730 🕐 Tue–Wed, Fri–Sun 10–6, Thu 10–9 🚇 U3 to Herrengasse 🦽 Good 🖐 Inexpensive

GLOBENMUSEUM

onb.ac.at

The historic globes in the collection of the Austrian National Library (in the same building as the Esperanto Museum, above) are unique. The oldest one dates back to 1536, but the most precious items are the 10 globes by Venetian Vicenzo Coronelli from the late 17th century. There are also globes featuring the moon and the planets.

🔢 E4 ✉ Mollard Palace, Herrengasse 9 ☎ 534 10 710 🕐 Tue–Wed, Fri–Sun 10–6, Thu 10–9 🦽 Good 🖐 Inexpensive

HAUS DER MUSIK

hausdermusik.com

The entrance to Vienna's sound museum reflects its playful and engaging approach, as visitors get to compose their own waltz, conduct, or play instruments. It is certainly a far cry from musty exhibits in glass cases; ideal for those with older childern.

🔢 F5 ✉ Seilerstätte 30 ☎ 513 48 50 🕐 Daily 10–10 🚇 U1, U2, U4 to Karlsplatz 🚊 Trams D, 2 to Schwarzenbergplatz 🦽 Good 🖐 Moderate; combined ticket with Mozarthaus

Inside Haus der Musik

An exhibit in the Globenmuseum

JESUITENKIRCHE

Italian-born Andrea Pozzo, a Jesuit brother, designed this beautiful, ornate church in the early 18th century. It belonged to the adjacent university, over which the Jesuits gained control in 1622. From this base the Jesuits drove forward the Counter-Reformation in Vienna.

G4 Dr-Ignaz-Seipel-Platz 1 512 52 320 Daily 7–7 U3 to Stubentor

LOBKOWITZ-PALAIS

theatermuseum.at

The present impressive facade is by Johann Bernhard Fischer von Erlach. Beethoven's Eroica Symphony was first performed here in 1804, and during the Congress of Vienna many famous balls were held. Today, the Austrian Theater Museum is here, hosting temporary exhibitions. The impressive facade is by Johann Bernhard Fischer von Erlach.

F5 Lobkowitzplatz 2 525 243 460 Wed–Mon 10–6 U1, U2, U4 to Karlsplatz/Oper Moderate

MOZARTHAUS

mozarthausvienna.at

Visit Mozart's lodgings where he wrote *The Marriage of Figaro*. No contemporary furniture has survived, but there is a vivid and entertaining presentation of his life and times. The audio guide includes examples of his music.

G4 Domgasse 5 512 17 91 Daily 10–7 Café on premises U1, U3 to Stephansplatz Good Moderate. Combined ticket includes Haus der Musik Museum shop

ÖSTERREICHISCHES POSTSPARKASSENAMT

A famous modernist building, the functionalism of Otto Wagner's Austrian Post Office Savings Bank (built 1910–12) made it seem ahead of its time. While it continues to operate as a bank, it also has a small museum about Otto Wagner.

H4 Georg-Coch-Platz 534 533 30 88 Mon-Fri 10am-5.30pm U1, U4 to Schwedenplatz Trams 1, 2 to Julius-Raab-Platz Moderate

One of Otto Wagner's Pavilions on Karlsplatz

The exterior of Mozarthaus

OTTO WAGNER PAVILLON

wienmuseum.at

Architect Otto Wagner designed the City Transit Railway. The finest stations are the two on Karlsplatz (1898) and the emperor's own at Schönbrunn. One of the Karlsplatz pavilions houses a museum dedicated to the architect.

⊞ F6 ⊠ Karlsplatz 🏛 Museum: Tue–Sun 10–6. Closed 1 Nov–31 Mar 🚇 U1, U2, U4 to Karlsplatz 💶 Museum: Inexpensive; free first Sun of month

PETERSKIRCHE

peterskirche.at

The most striking aspect of the lovely baroque St. Peter's Church is the way the architects, Gabriele Montani and Lukas von Hildebrandt, fitted it into a space so narrow that it looks almost as if it had been poured into a mold. Regular concerts are held here.

⊞ F4 ⊠ Petersplatz 6 ☎ 533 64 33 🕐 Mon–Fri 7am–8pm, Sat–Sun 9–9 🚇 U1, U3 to Stephansplatz 🚌 Hopper 2A 🚹 Few 💶 Free

The Strauss Monument in Stadtpark

STAATSOPER

wiener-staatsoper.at

The State Opera, which closed in 1944, reopened in 1955 with a performance of Beethoven's *Fidelio*. It remains one of the world's top opera stages. There are guided tours as well as performances.

⊞ F5 ⊠ Opernring 2 ☎ 51 444 22 50, tours: 51 444 26 14 🕐 Entrance by guided tour only. Tours in English at 2 and 3 🚇 U1, U2, U4 to Oper

STADTPARK

Laid out in 1863 on the old River Wien causeway, this very pleasant piece of city greenery covering 699, 654sq ft (65,000sq m) was laid out as an English landscape park, fashionable in the late 19th century. The park is dotted with monuments to the composers and artists of 19th-century Vienna. The most famous of them all is the striking 1903 Strauss Denkmal sporting a golden Strauss and an audience scantily clad, art nouveau onlookers.

⊞ G5 ⊠ Stubenring 🕐 Daily 8am–dusk 🚇 U3 to Stubentor, U4 to Stadtpark

UHRENMUSEUM

wienmuseum.at

The first of its kind in the world, the Clock Museum covers three floors of the Obizzi Palace and houses more than 3,000 exhibits from the 15th to the 20th centuries. Many are unique, including the "zappler"– a tiny clock that can be covered with a thimble.

⊞ F4 ⊠ Schulhof 2 (alley flanking Am Hof church) ☎ 533 22 65 🕐 Tue–Sun 10–6 🚇 U1, U3 to Stephansplatz 🚌 Hopper 2A 🚹 None 💶 Moderate; free first Sun of month ❓ Tours

Old Vienna Walk

A walk round the historic Innere Stadt gives you the chance to see some of Vienna's best-known sights and linger in its coffeehouses.

DISTANCE: 2.2 miles (3.5km) **ALLOW:** 2 hours

START

BURGRING
🚇 E5 Ⓜ U3 to Volkstheater

❶ Start at the Burgtor on the Ringstrasse. Walk through this triumphal arch into the Heldenplatz. On your right is the Neue Hofburg, containing the National Library and two museums.

❷ Continue through the arches into the main courtyard ("In der Burg") of the Hofburg (▷ 26–27). Through the Schweizertor (Swiss Gate) on the south side, the Burgkapelle and the sacred and profane treasuries (Schatzkammer) are reached.

❸ From the main courtyard approach the Michaelertor and the entrance to the Imperial Apartments. Exiting onto Michaelerplatz, turn right for Josefsplatz.

❹ Head along Augustinerstrasse, passing the Augustinerkirche (▷ 32), then the Albertina (▷ 32), on your right. Behind the Staatsoper (▷ 35) you will see Hotel Sacher (▷ 112).

END

BURGRING

❽ Proceed along the Heidenschuss through the Freyung (▷ 25), and turn left through the Ferstel arcade. Emerging on Herrengasse, walk back (left) to the Hofburg's Michaelertor.

❼ Walk west along the Graben past the Plague Column and the Peterskirche (▷ 35) down an alley on your right. Continue west along picturesque Naglergasse to the southwestern edge of Am Hof.

❻ Then turn left into Seilerstätte and left again into Himmelpfort-gasse. At Kärntner Strasse turn right and continue to Stephansplatz and St. Stephen's Cathedral (▷ 31). Opposite is the modern Haas-Haus (1990), by Hans Hollein.

❺ Beyond it turn left into Kärntner Strasse, Vienna's premier shopping precinct. Turn right down Annagasse, for the baroque Annakirche (▷ 32).

Shopping

ALTMANN & KÜHNE

altmann-kuehne.at

Altmann & Kühne are widely recognized as the makers of Vienna's best choco-lates and the most creative candy. There's something exquisitely Viennese about these tiny boxes containing delicious, high-end treats.

➕ F4 ✉ Graben 30 ☎ 533 09 27
🕐 Mon–Fri 9-6.30, Sat 10–5 🚇 U1, U3 to Stephansplatz

AUGARTEN

augarten.at

The finest Viennese porcelain is made at a small factory in the Augarten and the flagship store is the place to head to admire and buy. Augarten makes modern pieces as well as sets whose design dates back to the Habsburgs.

➕ F4 ✉ Spiegelgasse 3 ☎ 512 14 94
🕐 Mon–Sat 10–6 🚇 U1, U3 to Stephansplatz

DERBY-HANDSCHUHE

derby-handschuhe-wien.at

Derby devotes all its efforts to the production of the humble glove. The fact that this store remains in business may have something to do with Viennese winters though they also make gloves suitable to wear to the opera.

➕ F5 ✉ Plankengasse 5 ☎ 512 57 03
🕐 Mon–Fri 10–6, Sat 10–5 🚇 U1, U3 to Stephansplatz

DOBLINGER

doblinger.at

This is an unmissable shop for anyone with an interest in music. A music wonderland, you can pick up notes, books, instruments and CDs and the knowledgeable staff are happy to help.

➕ F4 ✉ Dorotheergasse 10 ☎ 515 030
🕐 Mon–Fri 10am–6pm, Sat 10am–1pm
🚇 U1, U3 to Stephansplatz

DOROTHEUM

dorotheum.com

This auction house was founded in the early 18th century in an old convent. You can find everything from the worthless to the priceless.

➕ F5 ✉ Dorotheergasse 17 ☎ 515 600
🕐 Art auctions: See website. Exhibitions of objects: Mon–Fri 10–6, Sat 9–5 🚇 U1, U2, U4 to Karlsplatz/Oper

FRICK AM GRABEN

This old bookshop, with four branches in Vienna, has been offering volumes off all kinds since 1875. There's a small English section and its selection of traditional children's books is very good.

➕ F4 ✉ Graben 27 ☎ 533 99 140
🕐 Mon–Fri 9–7, Sat 9.30–6 🚇 U1, U3 to Stephansplatz

GALERIE HEIKE CURTZE

heikecurtze.com

This Heike Curtze Gallery sells works by some of Austria's most prominent con-temporary artists. You can view the ceramics, oils, sculptures and collage on the website. Prices are very high.

➕ G5 ✉ Seilerstätte 15 ☎ 512 93 75
🕐 Tue–Fri 12–7, Sat 12–4 🚇 U1, U3 to Stephansplatz

GALERIE WOLFRUM

The olde-worlde specialist shop stocks a fine selection of art books, prints, post-cards and art. The print section is

---

BOOK TRADE

Austria imposes *Mehrwerts-teuer* (Value Added Tax) on books, which makes foreign paperbacks very expensive. Expect prices at least 50 percent above what you'd pay for a book in your own home town, and even more for newspapers.

particularly good with reproductions of Vienna's best-known artists.

F5 ⊠ Augustinerstrasse 10 ☎ 512 53 980 Mon–Fri 10–6, Sat 10–5 U1, U2, U4 to Karlsplatz/Oper

HAAS & HAAS

haas-haas.at

This upper-crust tea emporium prides itself on selling the finest leaves in black and green versions, plus other specialty coffee and cocoa. There are over 300 types to choose from, and there's a teahouse where you can sip them.

F5 ⊠ Stephansplatz 4 ☎ 512 97 70 Shop: Mon–Fri 9–6.30, Sat 9–6. Teahouse: Mon–Fri 8–8, Sat 8–6.30, Sun 9–6 U1, U3 to Stephansplatz

J. & L. LOBMEYR

lobmeyr.at

The famous glassware is still made to the 19th-century neo-baroque and neo-Renaissance design. Above the family-run shop is a small exhibition of J. & L. Lobmeyr's early work.

F5 ⊠ Kärntner Strasse 26 ☎ 512 05 08 Mon–Fri 10–7, Sat 10–6 U1, U3 to Stephansplatz

JULIUS MEINL AM GRABEN

meinlamgraben.at

Meinl is the city's finest grocer, offering a superb delicatessen counter, a café, bars and a pricey restaurant (check online for opening times). The store sells everything from Austrian Alpine cheese to local mustard.

F4 ⊠ Graben 19 ☎ 532 33 34 Mon–Fri 8–7.30, Sat 9–6 U1, U3 to Stephansplatz

KNIZE

knize.at

Knize is an exclusive men's tailors with branches in Vienna and Prague, but the shop is worth a look even if you aren't clothes shopping, as the 1913 building was designed by Adolf Loos.

F4 ⊠ Graben 13 ☎ 512 21 19 Mon–Fri 9.30–6, Sat 10–5 U1, U3 to Stephansplatz

KÖCHERT

koechert.at

Jewelers to the royal and imperial court since 1814, this reputable shop is elegant and restrained. Designs take inspiration from the imperial past and the early 20th century. Prices are as astronomical as you might expect.

F5 ⊠ Neuer Markt 15 ☎ 512 58 28 Mon–Fri 10–6, Sat 10–5 U1, U3 to Stephansplatz

METZGER

This famous shop specializes in candles, as well as honey cakes, gingerbread, chocolates and other aromatic gift items, most of which are hand-made.

F4 ⊠ Stephansplatz 7 ☎ 512 34 33 Mon–Fri 9–7, Sat 9–6 U1, U3 to Stephansplatz

MÜHLBAUER

muehlbauer.at

This flagship shop sells the distinctive Mühlbauer hats favored by Brad Pitt and

---

SACHERTORTE

The origin of Sachertorte, the chocolate cake for which the city is renowned, is so hotly disputed that there have been lawsuits between rival claimants. Those who want authenticity buy at Café Sacher (▷ 43; they will also mail). Hotel Imperial (▷ 112) also offers (to a different recipe) an Imperialtorte. Or you can buy a perfectly acceptable Sachertorte for much less at any branch of the Aida chain of cafés (▷ 43).

Madonna as well as lots of other stylishly designed headgear.

🔲 F4 ✉ Seilergasse 10 ☎ 512 22 41
🕙 Mon–Fri 10–6.30, Sat 10–6 🚇 U1, U3 to Stephansplatz

ÖSTERREICHISCHE WERKSTÄTTEN
austrianarts.com

A very famous and popular shop among art-loving Viennese, the Werkstätten offer glass ornaments and gifts, jewelry, accessories and things for the home, all with Secessionist designs.

🔲 F4 ✉ Kärntner Strasse 6 ☎ 512 24 18
🕙 Mon–Fri 10–7, Sat 10–6 🚇 U1, U3 to Stephansplatz

PINOCCHIO

A wonderful place to take young children, this upscale toy emporium stocks a wide selection of children's gifts crafted from wood, including toys, clocks and picture frames.

🔲 F5 ✉ Augustinerstrasse 7 ☎ 6991 954 71 02 🕙 Daily 10–6 🚇 U1, U2, U4 to Karlsplatz/Oper 🚋 Trams 1, 2, D to Opernring

ROBERT HORN
rhorns.com

If you are in the market for some high-quality leather goods, look no further than Robert Horn, a cult shop offering fine briefcases, handbags, wallets, belts and much more besides. There are also lots of relatively inexpensive accessories.

🔲 F4 ✉ Herrengasse 6–8 ☎ 513 82 94
🕙 Mon–Fri 10–6.30, Sat 10–5 🚇 U1, U3 to Stephansplatz

SHAKESPEARE & COMPANY
shakespeare.co.at

For some holiday reading look no further than this English-language book-store where you can pick up paperbacks

as well as guidebooks and Vienna-themed volumes.

🔲 F3 ✉ Sterngasse 2 ☎ 535 50 53
🕙 Mon–Sat 9–9 🚇 U1, U4 to Schwedenplatz

STEFFL
kaufhaus-steffl.at

This futuristic department store is crammed with designer labels. When you are done emptying your bank account, reteat to the café, bar and restaurant, which have some of the best views in the city.

🔲 F5 ✉ Kärntner Strasse 19 ☎ 930 560
🕙 Mon–Fri 10–8, Sat 9.30–6 🚇 U1, U3 to Stephansplatz

WIENER INTERIEUR

This wonderful shop specializes in reproductions of art deco jewelry as well as producing some of its own original pieces.

🔲 F4 ✉ Dorotheergasse 14 ☎ 512 28 98
🕙 Mon–Fri 10–6, Sat 10–1 🚇 U1, U2, U4 to Karlsplatz/Oper

WOKA
woka.at

A high-quality workshop selling furniture, art and lamps in the vein of Wiener Werkstätte.

🔲 G4 ✉ Singerstrasse 16 ☎ 513 29 12
🕙 Mon–Fri 10–6, Sat 10–5 🚇 U1, U3 to Stephansplatz

ANTIQUES SHOPS

Antiques shops are concentrated in the side streets running from Graben to the Hofburg. In the Bräunerstrasse, Dorotheergasse and Spiegelgasse, you will find an ever-changing display of what has survived from the collections of the Viennese art-loving middle class and nobil-ity. The Dorotheum (▷ 38) holds auctions.

Entertainment and Nightlife

BADESCHIFF WIEN

badeschiff.at

Forget the ocean cruise: Vienna has its very own ship pool in the Donaukanal, downstream from Schwedenplatz. The boat is narrow but 98ft (30m) long, and has an outdoor pool that is open through the summer. Day or two-hour tickets are available. The ship also holds a restaurant.

➕ H3 ✉ Franz-Josefs-Kai between Schwedenplatz and Urania 🕐 Pool: Summer 8am–midnight 🚇 U1, U4 to Schwedenplatz 🚋 Trams 1, 2 to Schwedenplatz

EDEN BAR

edenbar.at

An elegant dress code and live music are characteristic of this exclusive bar in the shadow of St. Stephen's. It's a popular venue among Vienna's high society.

➕ F4 ✉ Liliengasse 2 ☎ 512 74 50 🕐 Thu–Sat 10pm–4am 🚇 U1, U3 to Stephansplatz

ETABLISSEMENT RONACHER

musicalvienna.at

This variety theater, with a late 19th-century interior, has a broad program of events, with anything from a spectacular à la André Heller to a Broadway musical.

➕ G5 ✉ Seilerstätte 9 ☎ 588 85 🕐 Box office: Mon–Sat 10–1, 2–6, Sun 2–6. No shows on Wednesdays 🚇 U1, U3 to Stephansplatz, U4 to Stadtpark

KAMMERSPIELE

josefstadt.org

This subsidiary stage of the Theater in der Josefstadt (▷ 61) puts on plays—often comedies and farces, and popular Broadway hits.

➕ G4 ✉ Rotenturmstrasse 20 ☎ 42 700 300 tickets with credit card 🚇 U1, U4 to Schwedenplatz

KURSALON

kursalonwien.at

The Strauss summer festival takes place at the stunning Kursalon in the Stadtpark (originally a place where bourgeois park visitors could take the spa water). It hosts other classical music events throughout the year as well.

➕ G5 ✉ Johannesgasse 33 ☎ 512 57 90 🚇 U4 to Stadtpark 🚋 Tram 2 to Weihburggasse

NIGHTFLY'S CLUB

nightflys.at

An intimate American cellar bar where you'll hear golden oldies, from Glenn Miller to Frank Sinatra.

➕ F4 ✉ Dorotheergasse 14 ☎ 512 99 79 🕐 Summer daily 6pm–3am; winter 8pm–3am 🚇 U1, U3 to Stephansplatz

ÖSTERREICHISCHES FILMMUSEUM

filmmuseum.at

The dedicated Austrian Film Museum has kept this shrine to the movies alive. It screens Austrian and other films, with the theme changing monthly.

➕ F5 ✉ Augustinerstrasse 1 (Albertina) ☎ 533 70 54 🕐 Films: Check website for show times. Bar: 10am–midnight 🚇 U1, U2, U4 to Karlsplatz/Oper

---

NIGHT MUSIC

In summer there is a jazz festival held partly in the Staatsoper (▷ 35), and there is an open-air festival on the Donauinsel (Danube Island) in July. Performances generally start at 9pm but check the current *Wien Programm* (available at all Tourist Information Bureaux). The Bermuda Dreieck (Bermuda Triangle, ▷ 13) is where you'll find independent bars, restaurants, clubs, beer cellars, live music and cabaret.

PORGY & BESS

porgy.at

A club that showcases jazz musicians from both Austria and the rest of the world. Performances usually start at 8 or 8.30pm (check website). Food is also available, with a comforting selection of burgers and mezze.

🔲 G4 ✉ Riemergasse 11 ☎ 512 88 11 🕐 Daily 5pm–late 🚇 U3 to Stubentor

ROTER ENGEL

roterengel.at

This venue exemplifies the best of the Bermuda Dreieck (Bermuda Triangle) area ▷ 13. It calls itself a *Wein und Lieder-bar* (wine and song bar) and serves wine with cheeses. It also has rhythm and blues and folk evenings.

🔲 G3 ✉ Rabensteig 5 ☎ 535 41 05 🕐 Daily 5pm–4am 🚇 U1, U4 to Schwedenplatz 🚃 Trams 1, 2 to Schwedenplatz

STAATSOPER

wiener-staatsoper.at

The Vienna State Opera (▷ 35) ranks among the world's top opera houses. Viennese music lovers can be merciless, and being director of the State Opera is reputedly a brutal job. Among those who have held the post are Gustav Mahler, Richard Strauss and Lorin Maazel. World War II bombs destroyed most of the interior but the staircase and the foyers have been restored.

🔲 F5 ✉ Opernring 2 ☎ 514 44 22 50; ticket info: 514 44 29 50 🚇 U1, U2, U4 to Karlsplatz/Oper 🚃 Trams 1, 2, 71, D, Badner Bahn to Kärntner Ring/Oper

STADTFEST

stadtfest-wien.at

On a weekend in spring, the Inner City (Innere Stadt) hosts a variety of different kinds of events connected with the Vienna City Festival.

🔲 F4 ✉ Inner City 🕐 One weekend in spring 🚇 U3 to Herrengasse

STRANDBAR HERRMANN

strandbarherrmann.at

Situated where the River Wien debouches into the Danube Canal, this beach club—Vienna's first—has deck-chairs, dining and DJ music in the evening. Its the perfect for a warm summer's night.

🔲 H3 ✉ Hermannová ☎ 0720/229 996 🕐 Apr–Sep daily 10am–2am 🚇 U1, U4 to Schwedenplatz 🚃 Trams 1, 2 to Julius-Raab-Platz

WIENER KAMMEROPER

theater-wien.at

This is a seedbed for talent for the Volksoper and Staatsoper opera houses, as well as venues abroad. The schedule includes many lesser-known operas. A small, intimate space.

🔲 G4 ✉ Fleischmarkt 24 ☎ Tickets 588 85 🚇 U1, U4 to Schwedenplatz 🚃 Trams 1, 2 to Schwedenplatz

MUSICAL TRADITION

Music has been part of the city's culture from earliest times. In the mid-18th century Haydn and then Mozart began to displace the long-dominant Italian composers in public esteem. The 19th century was also rich in musical talent, some of it imported (Beethoven, Brahms) but much home-grown (Schubert, Bruckner, Hugo Wolf, Strauss father and son and Mahler). Later, Arnold Schönberg pioneered the 12-tone system, while his erstwhile pupils, such as Alban Berg and Anton von Webern, made the "Second Viennese School" world famous.

PRICES

Prices are approximate, based on a
3-course meal for one person.

€€€	over €40
€€	€20–€40
€	under €20

AIDA (€)

aida.at

This is one of the cafés in the classic
chain known for its devotion to the
color pink—from the cakes to the staff
uniforms. Aida has been in the business
of treat production for over a century so
they're clearly doing something right.

🟦 F4 ✉ Singerstrasse 1 ☎ 512 29 77
🕐 Mon–Fri 7am–10pm, Sat–Sun 8am–
10pm 🚇 U1, U3 to Stephansplatz. Also at:
Bognergasse 3, Wollzeile 28, Rotenturm-
strasse 24

BADESCHIFF (€€)

badeschiff.at

Aboard the Badeschiff Wien (▷ 41),
the restaurant serves excellent cuisine at
reasonable prices. There's a bar on the
top deck and a disco below.

🟦 H3 ✉ Franz-Josefs-Kai between
Schwedenplatz and Urania ☎ 660 31 24 703
🕐 May to mid-Sep daily 10am–1am; mid-Sep
to Apr 6pm–1am 🚇 U1, U4 to Schwedenplatz
🚋 Trams 1, 2 to Schwedenplatz

BEIM CZAAK (€)

czaak.com

This classic Viennese Beisl has a simple
interior, classic local meat dishes on the
menu and a quieter, less touristy, feel
than some similar places in the city
center. The schnitzel and Tafelspitz
are excellent.

🟦 G4 ✉ Postgasse 15 ☎ 513 72 15
🕐 Mon–Sat 4pm–11.30pm 🚇 U1, U4 to
Schwedenplatz

BRISTOL LOUNGE (€€€)

bristolvienna.com

Many consider this elegant restaurant in
the Hotel Bristol to be the best in town,
with the finest Viennese cuisine. For
those on a tighter budget try the set
lunch menu for €24.

🟦 F5 ✉ Mahlerstrasse 2 ☎ 515 16 553
🕐 Daily 7pm–midnight 🚇 U1, U2, U4 to
Karlsplatz/Oper

CAFÉ CENTRAL (€€)

palaisevents.at

A popular café and restaurant in the
Palais Ferstel (▷ 25), Café Central,
complete with marble columns and
vaulted ceilings, has a reasonably
priced lunch menu. There's a less
formal patisserie at Herrengasse 7.

🟦 E4 ✉ Corner of Herrengasse and
Strauchgasse ☎ 533 37 63 61 🕐 Mon–Sat
7.30am–10pm, Sun 10–10 🚇 U3 to
Herrengasse

CAFÉ DIGLAS (€)

diglas.at

Founded in 1923, Diglas was a
comparative latecomer to the coffeehouse scene. Its most famous regular
customer was Franz Lehár who most

FOOD FROM AROUND THE WORLD

Although Vienna has had a large
international community since the 1970s,
the choice of non-Viennese cooking is
not great. Pizza and pasta are ubiquitous,
and the number of Chinese and Japanese
restaurants is growing, with sushi becoming
increasingly popular; yet there are
surprisingly few French restaurants of
repute, the Greek and Spanish selection
is disappointing, and the cuisines of some
other territories are virtually unknown.

definitely snacked on Diglas' famous apple strudel. There's live piano music in the evenings, Thursdays to Saturdays.

➕ G4 ✉ Wollzeile 10 ☎ 512 57 65
🕐 Daily 8am–10.30pm 🚇 U1, U3
to Stephansplatz

CAFÉ PRÜCKEL (€€)

prueckel.at

Located on the *ringstrasse,* this classic, old-school coffeehouse specializes in traditional Viennese cooking as well as keeping punters well-supplied with coffee and cakes. It has one of the best interiors and ambiences of any of Vienna's grand cafés.

➕ G4 ✉ Stubenring 24 ☎ 512 61 15
🕐 Daily 8.30am–10pm 🚇 U3 to Stubentor
🚋 Tram 2 to Stubentor

CAFÉ SACHER (€€)

sacher.com

The ultimate in café elegance, this is where the Sachertorte, Austria's most famous gateau, was first created. Done out in the colors of the Austrian flag, with lots of tinkling crystal, this is an unmissable experience while in the Austrian capital.

➕ F5 ✉ Philharmonikerstrasse 4 ☎ 51 456 1053 🕐 Daily 8am–midnight 🚇 U1, U2, U4 to Karlsplatz/Oper

DEMEL (€€–€€€)

demel.at

Founded in 1786, the business was taken over by Christoph Demel in 1857 and remained in the family until Anna Demel's death in 1956. The staff are decked out in black uniforms with white frills. The lavish interior is a restoration dating from the 1930s.

➕ F4 ✉ Kohlmarkt 14 ☎ 535 17 170
🕐 Daily 9–7 🚇 U3 to Herrengasse
🚌 Bus 2A to Michaelerplatz

DO & CO (€€€)

doco.com

The restaurant's superb location in Hans Hollein's Haas Haus offers a view of the cathedral from the best tables. The excellent cuisine includes Far and Middle Eastern cooking mixed with local tradition.

➕ F4 ✉ Stephansplatz 12 ☎ 535 39 69
🕐 Daily 12–3, 6–midnight 🚇 U1, U3 to Stephansplatz

ESTERHAZYKELLER (€)

esterhazykeller.at

The Esterhazys gave free wine to the populace here during the 1683 Turkish siege. The wine is no longer free but it's still very good value serving simple food.

➕ F4 ✉ Haarhof 1 (off Wallnerstrasse)
☎ 533 34 82 🕐 Mon–Fri 5pm–midnight, Sat–Sun 11am–midnight 🚇 U3 to Herrengasse

FABIOS (€€€)

fabios.at

When it first opened, Fabio Giacobello's designer restaurant became the most fashionable of Vienna's top-level eateries almost overnight. Its creative cuisine has made it a celebrity hot spot.

➕ F4 ✉ Tuchlauben 4–6 ☎ 532 22 22 🕐 Mon–Sat 9am–11pm 🚇 U1, U3 to Stephansplatz

FIGLMÜLLER (€€)

figlmuller.at

Figlmüller is known for one dish—its unsurpassed schnitzel, plate-covering wheels of thinly cut veal, fried in bread-crumbs and served with a slice of lemon. Nowhere does them better, but it also serves other Viennese dishes as well as local wine.

➕ G4 ✉ Wollzeile 5 (also at Bäckerstrasse 6) ☎ 512 61 77 🕐 Sep–July daily 11–10 🚇 U1, U3 to Stephansplatz

INNERE STADT WHERE TO EAT

HEINER (€€)

heiner.co.at

The branch overlooking Kärntner Strasse is excellent, but the little Biedermeier interior of Heiner in the Wollzeile is irresistible. The cakes and pastries are superb and the coffee good; there are fine handmade chocolates, too.

⊞ F5 ✉ Kärntner Strasse 21–3 ☎ 512 68 63 🕓 Mon–Sat 8.30–7.30, Sun 10–7.30 🚇 U1, U3 to Stephansplatz

KERN'S BEISL (€€)

kernbeisl.at

If you want to sample real Austrian cooking, look no further than this wonderful Beisl where time seems to have stood still circa 1950. It's unpretentious but serves excellent food and a wide selection of Austrian wines by the glass.

⊞ F4 ✉ Kleeblattgasse 4 (off Tuchlauben) ☎ 533 91 88 🕓 Mon–Sat 9am–11pm 🚇 U1, U3 to Stephansplatz

KORNAT (€€–€€€)

kornat.at

For over 25 years this Croatian eatery has been serving fish flown in fresh from the Dalmatian coast with wines from Hvar and Korcula. The interior is crisp and modern, the service brisk.

⊞ G3 ✉ Marc-Aurel-Strasse 8 ☎ 535 65 18 🕓 Daily 11.30am–midnight 🚇 U1, U4 to Schwedenplatz

MEINL AM GRABEN (€€€)

meinlamgraben.at

At a discreet gourmet stop in the quality grocer Meinl you can enjoy the best of Austrian cooking in an informal atmosphere and fabulous wines.

⊞ F4 ✉ Graben 19 ☎ 532 33 346 000 🕓 Mon–Wed 8.30am–midnight, Thu–Fri 8am–midnight, Sat 9am–midnight 🚇 U3, U1 to Stephansplatz

PLACHUTTA (€€€)

plachutta.at

One of several Plachutta restaurants, the real draw at the Wollzeile branch is the Tafelspitz (boiled beef), served in its own broth. The interior is modern and the location great for people watching.

⊞ G4 ✉ Wollzeile 38 ☎ 512 15 77 🕓 Daily 11.30am–midnight 🚇 U3 to Stubentor 🚋 Tram 2 to Stubentor

RESTAURANT LALE (€€)

lale.at

This popular Middle Eastern restaurant specializes in oversized kebabs and grilled meats, fresh pita bread and satisfying sides like tzatziki and hummus.

⊞ G4 ✉ Franz-Josefs-Kai 29 ☎ 535 27 36 🕓 Daily 11.30am–midnight 🚇 U1, U4 to Schwedenplatz

WRENKH (€€)

wrenkh-wien.at

Exquisite vegetarian cuisine with choices such as wild rice risotto with mushrooms, and Greek fried rice with vegetables, sheep's cheese and olives.

⊞ F4 ✉ Bauernmarkt 10 ☎ 533 15 26 🕓 Mon–Sat 11–11 🚇 U1, U3 to Stephansplatz

STREET EATS

The most popular quick bite is *würst* (sausage). Stands typically serve hot dogs, German-style sausages and a uniquely Austrian invention: *käsekrainer* (grilled pork stuffed with cheese). On ordering a sausage, you'll be asked "sweet *(süss)* or spicy *(scharf)*?," referring to the type of mustard. In recent years, Middle Eastern doner kebab stands have sprung up, offering satisfying sandwiches of spicy lamb, veal or chicken. Some of the best kebabs are at Restaurant Lale (▷ above).

Ringstrasse

Largely undamaged by World War II, the Ringstrasse is one of Europe's great boulevards. It has many magnificent buildings created for cultural and political institutions, as well as elegant parks.

Top 25

Akademie der Bildenden Künste	**50**
Burgtheater	**51**
Kunsthistorisches Museum	**52**
MuseumsQuartier	**54**
Rathaus	**55**
Secession	**56**
More to See	**57**
Walk	**59**
Shopping	**60**
Entertainment and Nightlife	**61**
Where to Eat	**62**

3

4

5

6

7

Wickenburggasse

Schössergasse

Jugend-
gerichtshof

Arbeits- und
Sozialgericht

LANDESGERICHTSSTRASSE

Schön-
bornpark

Florianigasse

Lange Gasse

Lammgasse

Tulpengasse

Friedr
Shmr
Pla

Rathaus

Lenaugasse

Piaristen-
keller

Piaristen-
kirche

Maria-Treu-
Kloster

Piaristengasse

Theater in der
Josefstadt

Kabarett
Niedermair

Josefstädter Strasse

**JOSEFSTADT
8**

Pfeilgasse

Strozzigasse

Zeltgasse

Piaristengasse

Neudeggergasse

Lange Gasse

Vienna's English Theatre

Josefsgasse

Trautsongasse

AUERSPERGSTRASSE

Palais
Auersperg

MU
STRA

LERCHENFELDER STRASSE

Weghuber-
Park

Lerchengasse

gasse

NEUSTIFTGASSE

Zieglergasse

Myrthengasse

Neubaugasse

NEUSTIFTGASS

th

St Ulrich

Kirchenc
gasse

Gutenbergg
Spitelberg

Karl-Farkas-
Park

BURGGASSE

Atelier-
theater

Bandgasse

Stuckgasse

BURGGASSE

Sigmundgasse

stiftgasse

Kandlgasse

Westbahnstrasse

St Laurenz

Zieglergasse

Hermanngasse

Kosmos
Theater

Renaissance
Theater

Kirchengasse

Siebensterngasse

stiftgasse

Mondscheingasse

Lindengasse

Neubaugasse

Mariah

Stiftskirc

Neubaugasse

Seidengasse

Stollgasse

Lindengasse

Richtergasse

Andreasgasse

Neubaugasse

Zollergasse

Maria-Hilf-Kloster

Barnabitengasse

Hofmobiliendepot

Zieglergasse

Bundes-
länderplatz

Schadekgasse

**Haus des
Meeres**

Fritz-
Grünbaum
Platz

Luftbadga

Esterhazy-
Park

Amerlingstrasse

Esterhazy-

Otto-Bauer-gasse

Schmalzhofgasse

Königseggasse

GUMPENDORFER STRASSE

Cornelius gasse

Dürergasse

WIENZEILE

Falco-
stiege

Kaunitzgasse

LINKE

HAMBUR

Laquai-
platz

TAG

HOFMÜHLGASSE

0   250 m

0   250 yds

B

C

D

Grillparzerstrasse

Museum auf
Abruf

...lderstrasse

Wiener Stadt-
und Landesbib...

Rathaus

Rathaus-
platz

UNIVERSITÄTSRING

Löwelstrasse

Burgtheater

Meinrad-
platz

Rathaus-
Park

Reichsrats-...
strasse

...gasse

Schottenstift

Kaiserin
Elisabeth
Denkmal

DR K-RENNER-
RING

Parlament

Volksgarten

Löwelstrasse

Ballhaus-
platz

...mmeringplatz

Palais
Epstein

VOLKSGARTEN-
STRASSE

Erzherzog-
Karl-Denkmal

...stiz-
...alast

Helden-
platz

BELLARIASTRASSE

BURGRING

Prinz-Eugen-
Denkmal

Volks-
theater

**Natur-
historisches
Museum**

Maria-Theresien-
platz

Burgtor
(Heldentor)

Architektur-
zentrum

MUSEUMSPLATZ

**Kunsthistorisches
Museum**

...unsthalle
Wien

MUMOK

BABENBERGERSTRASSE

OPERNRING

MuseumsQuartier

Eschenbachgasse

Elisabethstrasse

Leopold Museum

ZOOM
Kindermuseum

Museumsquartier

Nibelungengasse

OPERNGASSE

Dschungel
Wien

Rahlgasse

GETREIDE-
MARKT

**Akademie
der Bildenden
Künste**

Schwaighofer-
gasse

Theo-
baldgasse

FRIEDRICHSTRASSE

...t Joseph

...kulttheater

Gasse

Lehár-

gasse

Secession

Karlsplatz

Filgrader

Laim-
grubengasse

Girardigasse

**Theater an
der Wien**

Kunsthalle Wien
project space

...MPENDORFER
STRASSE

Alfred-
Grünwald-
Park

Kösterigasse

Naschmarkt

WIENZEILE

...streingeng...

Wagner
Apartments

RECHTE

...ckenbrückengasse

...ASSE

E   **F**

Akademie der Bildenden Künste

TOP 25

Otto Wagner's apartment (left); Schiller statue (middle); exterior (right)

THE BASICS

akbild.ac.at
+ E6
✉ Schillerplatz 3
☎ 588 162 201
🕐 Tue–Sun 10–6
Ⓜ U1, U2, U4 to Karlsplatz/Oper
🚋 Trams 1, 2 to Babenberger Strasse
♿ Call in advance for access at Makartgasse entrance
✋ Moderate
❓ Audio guide

HIGHLIGHTS

● *Last Judgment*, Hieronymus Bosch
● *Views of Venice*, Antonio Guardi
● *Family in a Courtyard*, Pieter de Hooch
● *Sketches for Banqueting House, Whitehall*, Rubens

Famous for rejecting one Adolf Hitler as a student in 1907, the Academy of Fine Arts is thankfully associated with more celebrated names such as Otto Wagner, Friedensreich Hundertwasser and many others. The gallery specializes in old European masters but the building itself is worth seeing on its own.

The building The academy was completed in 1876 by one of the greatest architects of the Ringstrassen era, Theophil Hansen, whose other work includes the classical Parliament, the Stock Exchange and numerous neo-Renaissance palaces. In the middle of the square in front is a statue of the poet Friedrich Schiller (1759–1805). Along the facade are figures from antiquity associated with the fine arts; on the back are allegorical frescoes by August Eisenmenger. Founded in 1692 by the painter Peter von Strudel, the academy numbers among its alumni the painter Friedensreich Hundertwasser, whose spectacular multihued house at Löwengasse, 3rd District, is a tourist attraction, and Fritz Wotruba, designer of the 1976 Wotruba Kirche (▷ 101), an extraordinary concrete structure.

The interior Anselm Feuerbach's ceiling fresco, *Downfall of Titans*, dominates the Basilical Hall; the collection of Dutch Masters is renowned and the graphic art collection is superb. Few teaching academies possess such a large graphic collection developed over 300 years.

Exterior and auditorium of the Burgtheater

Burgtheater

The Burgtheater is one of the oldest in the world and Austria's national theater in all but name. It is regarded as one of the best German-language theaters.

Origins The name is taken from the court theater that stood on the edge of the Hofburg (on Michaelerplatz) from the time of ruler Maria Theresa (1741) until 1888.

Architecture This neo-Renaissance building by Karl von Hasenauer and Gottfried Semper opened in 1888, but it was soon altered; so much attention in the design had been paid to architectural proportion and so little to function that some of the boxes faced away from the stage and the acoustics were appalling. An anecdote claimed that "In the Parliament you can't hear anything, in the Rathaus you can't see anything and in the Burgtheater you can neither see nor hear anything."

Decorative plan Inside and out, the Burgtheater is a symbolic celebration of the history of drama. On the central facade are monuments to the world's greatest playwrights. The ceremonial stairways that rise through the two wings toward the auditorium hold busts of the great Austrian and German dramatists. Gustav Klimt, his brother Ernst and Franz von Matsch decorated the ceilings above the stairway with frescoes depicting the history of theater. Oil portraits of famous Viennese actors and actresses hang in the foyer.

THE BASICS

burgtheater.at

➕ E4

✉ Universitätsring 2

☎ 514 444 140

🕐 Backstage theater tours: Daily at 3pm. Closed Jul and Aug except for tours. No tours during afternoon performances

🚇 U2 to Schottentor

🚊 Trams 1, D to Burgtheater

♿ Good; by prior arrangement

💰 Moderate

HIGHLIGHTS

Exterior
● View from the Rathaus across Ringstrasse
Interior
● *Thespiscart*, Gustav Klimt
● *Globe Theatre, London*, Gustav Klimt
● *Theater at Taormina*, Gustav Klimt
● *Medieval Mystery Theater*, Ernst Klimt
● *Molière's Le Malade Imaginaire*, Ernst Klimt

Kunsthistorisches Museum

HIGHLIGHTS

● *The Tower of Babel*,
Brueghel
● *Madonna in the
Meadow*, Raphael
● *Infanta Margareta
Teresa*, Velázquez
● *Gold Salt Cellar*, Cellini

TIP

● Be sure to catch Antonio
Canova's dramatic *Theseus
and the Centaur* on the
grand staircase.

**In the Museum of Art History you'll
find the Habsburgs' fabulous collection,
acquired over centuries by archdukes
and emperors.**

Origins The German architect Gottfried
Semper planned to continue the sweep of the
Neue Hofburg and build a parallel wing on
the other side of the Heldenplatz; both wings
were to extend across the Ringstrasse, creating
a gigantic Imperial Forum of museums. The
Museum of Art History and Natural History
Museum (▷ 58) facing it are the partial
realization of this attempt to bring together the
widely dispersed Habsburg treasures. The
Museum of Art History contains collections
of paintings, Egyptian objects, sculpture,
decorative art, coins and medals.

Architectural decoration Both the Museum of Art History and the Natural History Museum opposite are principally the work of Gottfried Semper; their interiors are by Karl Hasenauer. Between the museums lies a park, dominated by a monument to Maria Theresa (1740–80). Inside the Museum of Art History, marble and stucco are interspersed with murals; most notable is the ceiling fresco above the main landing, Mihály Munkácsy's *Apotheosis of Art*. The dome has medallions of collector-emperors. Hasenauer planned showrooms appropriate to their contents: The Egyptian collection, for example, is ornamented with columns from Luxor, a present from the Khedive to the Emperor Franz Josef. Benvenuto Cellini's Saliera (*Salt Cellar*), completed in 1543, is a gem of Renaissance craftsmanship.

THE BASICS

khm.at
+ E5
⊠ Maria-Theresien-Platz
☎ 525 240
🕐 Tue–Sun 10–6 (Thu until 9). Closed 24 Dec, shorter hours 1 Jan
🍴 Café in Cupola Hall
🚇 U2 to Museums-Quartier, U3 to Volkstheater
🚃 Trams 1, 2, D to Burgring
♿ Good. Use the side entrance
💶 Expensive. Combined ticket with the Imperial Treasury (▷ 26–27)
❓ Frequent lectures and special exhibitions

MuseumsQuartier

Relaxing in the MuseumsQuartier

THE BASICS

mqw.at

+ D5

✉ Museumsplatz 1

☎ 523 588 117 31

🕐 Daily 10–6 (some museums 10–7), Thu 10–9

🚇 U2 to MuseumsQuartier, U2, U3 to Volkstheater

♿ Good

💰 Expensive (separate tickets); combined tickets available

❓ Information point, ticket office and shop at entrance

HIGHLIGHTS

● *Death and Life*, Gustav Klimt
● Self-portrait by Egon Schiele (both in the Leopold Museum)

TIP

● Enjoy excellent and tasty traditional Viennese fare at Glacis Beisl, with its open-air terrace and modern dining room. It is reached up two flights of steps at the rear of Museumplatz (☎ 526 56 60 🕐 Daily 11am–2am, kitchen until 11pm).

Museums in this quarter occupying the former Imperial Stables include the Kunsthalle and the Museum of Modern Art (MUseum MOderner Kunst or MUMOK). The Leopold Museum has fine works by Gustav Klimt, Egon Schiele and other artists of the period.

Meeting place Covering an impressive 968,759sq ft (90,000sq m), Vienna's Museum District should be near the top of every visitor's itinerary. The 60 cultural institutions here deal in everything from high-brow art to children's finger-paint workshops, street art to gastronomy events. It's one of the largest cultural spaces in the world and it's also a nightlife attraction among young people in particularly. It is one of the liveliest places in the city, as it's central and easy to access. Wien's young meet here to see the cutting-edge exhibitions in the Kunsthalle at its heart or simply to relax on the "Enzis" in the main courtyard—modernistic pieces of outdoor furniture on which you can lie, lean or sit.

The Leopold Museum Numerous cultural institutions, such as the Architekturzentrum, the Tanzquartier, the Children's Museum and the Museum of Modern Art, attract all kinds of visitors (some of them visit the MUMOK just for the fine view from its top floor). The flagship is definitely the Leopold Museum, with its excellent collection of Austrian fin-de-siècle art brought together and donated by the collector Rudolf Leopold (1925–2010).

A summer concert (left) in the courtyard of the Rathaus (right)

The "new" City Hall (neues Rathaus), built between 1872 and 1883 by architect Friedrich Schmidt, is possibly the finest neo-Gothic building in Vienna.

Inspiration The great buildings along the Ringstrasse, built between the 1860s and 1880s, exemplify the values of Liberalism—industrial modernization, democracy and capitalist enterprise. It is typically Viennese that this vision of the future was expressed in historic symbols. Schmidt chose as his model town halls typical of medieval Flanders. The main inspiration was the Brussels City Hall.

Inside and out The huge facade, with its traceried arches over the arcades, faces the Ringstrasse; above the arches are loggias and imposing balustrades adorned with statues. Rising from the middle is the 321ft (98m) tower topped by a 11ft (3.4m) copper statue. Inside, the grand staircases, noble promenades and richly decorated halls are spectacular; don't miss the City Council Chamber and the Ceremonial Hall.

City Council The members of City Hall have a surprising degree of authority. While many smaller decisions are made on the district or neighborhood level (Vienna is divided into 23 separate districts), City Hall controls the budgets for schools, maintenance and parks, among other important items. It also reserves the right to veto decisions taken at local level.

Secession

The Secession's dome of gilded laurel leaves (left); detail of the facade (right)

THE BASICS

secession.at

☐ E6

✉ Friedrichstrasse 12

☎ 587 53 07

🕐 Tue–Sun 10–6

🍴 Outside summer café

Ⓟ U1, U2, U4 to Karlsplatz

♿ Few

💰 Moderate

❓ Guided tours in English Sat 11am

HIGHLIGHTS

● Three carved gorgons over the doorway

● Inscription *Ver Sacrum* (Sacred Spring)

● Dome of gilded laurel leaves

● Picturesque sculpted owls

● Vast flower tubs on tortoise stands

● Statue: *Mark Antony in a Chariot Drawn by Lions* (1900), Arthur Strasser

● *Beethoven Frieze* (1902), Gustav Klimt

In a gesture of defiance toward the art establishment, this exhibition building of revolutionary design was built behind the Academy of Fine Arts. Its motto is inscribed over the entrance: "To every age its art, to art its freedom."

Vienna Secession In 1897, frustrated with the increasing conservatism of academic painting in Vienna and its stranglehold on the art market, a group of young artists broke away to form the subsequently famous "Vienna Secession." Its elected head was Gustav Klimt, whose *Beethoven Frieze*—an allegorical interpretation of the themes of the Ninth Symphony and a homage to the composer—can be seen here.

Jugendstil Klimt began his career working in the conventional genre of historical painting (exemplified by his work for the Burgtheater, ▷ 51). The Secession's style was associated with Jugendstil, the German version of art nouveau. It is sensuous and decorative, and achieves its best effects in architecture and stained glass.

The exhibition hall The breakaway artists needed a hall to exhibit their own works and to display avant-garde art from abroad. In 1898, Joseph Maria Olbrich completed the cube-like, towered and windowless Secession Building with a glass roof that provided daylight. The Viennese dubbed it the "Golden Cabbage" because of its gilded dome of laurel leaves.

More to See

HAUS DES MEERES

haus-des-meeres.at

The "Flakturm" in Esterhazypark, one of six World War II anti-aircraft towers, now houses crocodiles, snakes and spiders, as well as an aquarium. Views from the tower's outlook platform are impressive.
🔲 D6 ✉ Fritz-Grünbaum-Platz 1 (in Esterhazypark) ☎ 587 14 17 🕐 Daily 9–6 (Thu 9–9). Shark feeding: Mon 10.30am, Wed 3pm 🍴 Café 🚇 U3 to Neubaugasse 🚌 Buses 13A to Esterhazygasse/Haus des Meeres, 14A, 57A to Haus des Meeres 🚾 Good 🎫 Expensive

HOFMOBILIENDEPOT

hofmobiliendepot.at

This undervisited museum houses a collection of furniture made by craftsmen for their Habsburg patrons from the time of Maria Theresa onward. It's a must for anyone interested in antiques.
🔲 C6 ✉ Andreasgasse 7 ☎ 524 33 57 🕐 Tue–Sun 10–6 🚇 U3 to Zieglergasse 🚾 Good (use entrance on Andreasgasse) 🎫 Moderate

KAISERIN ELISABETH DENKMAL

This monument was erected in the Volksgarten following the assassination of the popular empress by an anarchist in Geneva in 1898.
🔲 E4 ✉ Volksgarten (Burgtheater end) 🚋 Trams 1, 2 to Burgtheater

NASCHMARKT

naschmarkt-vienna.com

This food market is a literal taste of the real Vienna and its two aisles are divided between restaurants and market stalls, selling everything from spices to fish. The two ends of Naschmarkt are marked by buildings of the Viennese Jugendstil: at Getreidemarkt to t he east is the Secession building (▷ 56) by Joseph Olbrich; and at Kettenbrückengasse to the west are two apartment buildings with floral ornaments by Otto Wagner.
🔲 E6 ✉ Wienzeile from Getreidemarkt to Kettenbrückengasse 🕐 Mon–Fri 6am–7.30pm, Sat 6–5 🚇 U4 to Kettenbrückengasse

Hammerhead shark in Haus des Meeres

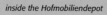

inside the Hofmobiliendepot

NATURHISTORISCHES MUSEUM

nhm-wien.ac.at

Exhibits here include dinosaur skeletons and the 25,000-year-old Venus of Willendorf statuette.

➕ E5 ✉ Maria-Theresien-Platz ☎ 521 770 🕐 Wed 9–9, Thu–Mon 9–6.30 🚇 U2 Volkstheater 🚋 Trams 1, 2, D to Burgring ♿ Good; use entrance at Burgring 7 💲 Moderate

PARLAMENT

parlament.gv.at

Visit the impressive marble hall and former Imperial Diet. The 1884 Historicist building was once the parliament of the western half of the Austro-Hungarian Empire. It was damaged by bombing during World War II; those areas accessible to the public were faithfully restored.

➕ D4 ✉ Dr-Karl-Renner-Ring 3 ☎ 40 110 24 00 🕐 Guided tours: mid-Sep to mid-Jul Mon–Thu 11, 2, 3, 4, Fri 11, 1, 2, 3, 4, Sat 11–4 hourly; mid-Jul to mid-Sep Mon–Sat 11–4 hourly (except 15 Aug). No tours when Parliament is sitting 🚇 U2, U3 to Volkstheater 🚋 Trams 1, 2, D to Parlament ♿ Good 💲 Inexpensive

THEATER AN DER WIEN

theater-wien.at

Original owner Emanuel Schikaneder, librettist for Mozart's *Magic Flute*, complained that he had written "such a good piece, but Mozart ruined it all with his music." A shrewd impresario, Schikaneder would have appreciated the theater's success with such musicals as *Cats*, which ran for 11 years.

➕ E6 ✉ Linke Wienzeile 6 ☎ 588 85 🕐 See events online, closed in summer 🚇 U1, U2, U4 to Karlsplatz

VOLKSGARTEN

bundesgaerten.at

Dominated by the Doric Theseus-Tempel, this public park is an oasis of tranquility in the heart of the city.

➕ E4 ✉ Dr-Karl-Renner-Ring 🕐 Daily May–Sep 6am–10pm; Oct–Apr 6am–9pm 🚇 U3 to Volksgarten 🚋 Trams 1, 2, D to Parlament

The Naturhistorisches Museum

Flowers bloom in Volksgarten

Ringstrasse Circle

A walk along Vienna's Ringstrasse, which encircles the historic old city, offers a panorama of Historicist buildings and elegant parks.

DISTANCE: 3 miles (5km) **ALLOW:** 3 hours

START

SCHWEDENPLATZ
🚊 G3/4 🚇 U1, U4 to Schwedenplatz

1 Walk along the Franz-Josefs-Kai westward from Schwedenplatz, then follow the Ring southward. On your right (in Deutschmeisterplatz) is the Rossauer Kaserne (once a barracks).

2 Almost immediately to your left is Theophil Hansen's graceful Börse (Stock Exchange). Continue across Schottentor. Set back on your right you will pass the Votivkirche (▷ 71), then the neo-Renaissance university.

3 Continue to the Burgtheater (▷ 51) opposite the Rathaus (City Hall, ▷ 55). Walk on past the Parlament (▷ 58) on your right, while to your left is the Volksgarten (▷ 58).

4 Continuing east on the Ring you reach on your right the Naturhistorisches Museum (▷ 58), the Kunsthistorisches Museum (▷ 52–53) and the monument to Maria Theresa.

END

SCHWEDENPLATZ

8 Finally you pass the former War Ministry, and follow the Ring round to its end, leaving the Urania cultural center on your right and returning to Schwedenplatz on Franz-Josefs-Kai.

7 Leave the Stadtpark at the east end near the Museum of Applied Art. Cross the Ringstrasse to Georg-Coch-Platz and walk past Otto Wagner's Austrian Post Office Savings Bank (▷ 34).

6 Continuing southeast on the Ring, you will see on your right the Hotel Imperial, then Schwarzenberg-platz. Next enter the Stadtpark (▷ 35) near the Strauss Monument (▷ 35).

5 Continue past Schillerplatz, with its statue to the poet Schiller in front of the Academy of Fine Arts, to the State Opera on your left (▷ 35).

Shopping

CHRISTKINDLMARKT

christkindlmarkt.at

This is the biggest of Vienna's Christmas markets, which run from mid-November until Christmas Eve. Popular goods include wooden crafts, sweets, leatherware and much more.

🔲 D4/E4 ☒ Rathausplatz ⓖ Mid-Nov to 24 Dec Sun–Thu 10–9.30, Fri–Sat 10–10 (24 Dec 10–6) 🚇 U2 to Rathaus 🚋 Trams 1, D to Rathausplatz

INA KENT WIEN

inakent.com

The name of the game here are boldly-designed leather goods such as handbags and belts. The maker's studio is situated within the shop. There's another branch at Siebensterngasse 50.

🔲 C6 ☒ Neubaugasse 34 ☎ 699 19 54 10 90 ⓖ Mon–Fri 11–7, Sat 11–6 🚇 U3 to Neubaugasse

NASCHMARKT

Vienna's gourmet market is definitely one of the Austrian capital's must-visits. Even if you don't buy any fresh produce you can sample its wares in the many small restaurants. A flea market is held next to it every Saturday from 6.30am to 6pm.

🔲 E6 ☒ Between the Linke and Rechte Wienzeile ⓖ Permanent market Mon–Fri 6am–7.30pm, Sat 6–5. Restaurants to 10pm 🚇 U4 to Kettenbrückengasse

NEUBAUGASSE

This fashionable side street in Vienna's 7th District offers an eclectic mix of shops with high-end fashion, second-hand clothing, books, music and cafés.

🔲 C6 ☒ Neubaugasse ⓖ Most shops: Mon–Fri 9–7, Sat 10–6 🚇 U3 to Neubaugasse 🚌 Bus 13A to Siebensterngasse; tram 46 to Strozzigasse

RAUMINHALT

rauminhalt.at

An unusual gallery/shop devoted to decorative objects and furniture of the last five decades. Plastic is particularly well represented, with the 1950s a specialty.

🔲 E6/E7 ☒ Schleifmühlgasse 13 ☎ 650 409 9892 ⓖ Tue–Fri 12–7, Sat 10–3 🚌 Bus 59A to Schleifmühl-gasse; tram 62 to Paulanergasse

RINGSTRASSEN-GALERIEN

ringstrassen-galerien.at

State-of-the-art shopping mall selling designer brands and gastronomic delicacies, from Asayake Sushi to Testa Rossa Coffee Bar.

🔲 F5 ☒ Kärntner Ring ⓖ Shops: Mon–Fri 10–7, Sat 10–6; restaurants: Daily 8am–1am 🚇 U1, U2, U4 to Karlsplatz 🚋 Trams 1, 2, D to Kärntner Ring/Oper

SPITTELBERG MARKET

All through the year local handicrafts are sold in the Spittelberg area in small shops, but before Christmas there is a street market.

🔲 D5 ☒ Spittelberggasse ⓖ Mid-Nov to 23 Dec Mon–Fri 2–9, Sat–Sun 10–9 🚇 U3 to Neubaugasse 🚋 Tram 49 to Stiftgasse

SZÁSZI HÜTE

szaszi.com

This traditional hatmaker's was established in 1858 and little has changed here since. It's one of a dying breed but continues to produce handmade hats your great-grandfather might have worn. If you are serious about buying a hat, you can even make an appointment for a Sunday fitting.

🔲 E6 ☒ Mariahilferstrasse 4 ☎ 522 56 52 ⓖ Mon–Wed 10–6, Thu–Fri 10–12.30 🚇 U2 to MuseumsQuartier

Entertainment and Nightlife

BARFLY'S CLUB
barflys.at

A Vienna original, this cocktail bar was founded in 1989 by Mario Castillo from the Dominican Republic. It's still as popular as it was back then and mixes some of the best long drinks on the Danube.

➕ D5 ✉ Esterhazygasse 33 ☎ 586 0825
🚇 U3 to Neubaugasse61

BURGKINO
burgkino.at

This small foreign-language cinema keeps its finger on the pulse with screenings of the latest movies from Europe and beyond. It's a great opportunity to see incredible films that don't make the local multiplex back home.

➕ E5 ✉ Opernring 19 ☎ 587 84 06
🚇 U1, U2, U4 to Karlsplatz/Oper

CAMERA CLUB
camera-club.at

Old-school 1970s rock and music club which still draws leading national and international club bands. The best nights are Fridays and Saturdays. The rest of the week brings mainly DJs and dancing. At weekends, doors open at 11pm and the party goes on till the morning.

➕ C6 ✉ Neubaugasse 2 ☎ 523 30 63
🕐 Mon–Thu 7pm–2am, Fri–Sat 11pm–6am
🚇 U3 to Neubaugasse

DSCHUNGEL WIEN
dschungelwien.at

Bang in the heart of the Museums-Quartier, this children's theater has the full range to keep the kids entertained, from puppets to dance, theater to music. There's also a café and adults pay kids' prices for matinees.

➕ D5 ✉ Museumsplatz 1 ☎ 522 07 20 20
🚇 U2 to MuseumsQuartier

FLEX
flex.at

One of downtown Vienna's best spots for DJs nights and live concerts. Even after all these years its still exudes an alternative flair.

➕ F2 ✉ At the Danube Canal, downstairs from Augartenbrücke ☎ 533 75 25 🕐 Daily 9pm–4am 🚇 U2, U4 to Schottenring

PAVILLON IM VOLKSGARTEN
volksgarten-pavillon.at

A café by day and a disco with an open-air dance floor by night, this is one of Vienna's most popular places to head when the sun goes down.

➕ E4 ✉ Burgring 1 ☎ 532 09 07 🕐 Apr to mid-Sep daily 11am–2am 🚇 U3 to Volkstheater 🚋 Trams 1, 2, D to Dr-Karl-Renner-Ring

THEATER IN DER JOSEFSTADT
josefstadt.org

Close to Viennese hearts, this theater was once the powerhouse of the player-director Max Reinhardt. It was built in 1788 and renovated by Joseph Kornhäusel in neoclassical style in the 1820s. Outside, plaques honor Reinhardt and Hugo von Hofmannsthal. Jugendstil drama is still played and promoted here.

➕ C4 ✉ Josefstädterstrasse 26 ☎ 42 700 300 🚇 U2 to Rathaus 🚋 Trams 2, 46 to Lederergasse/Strozzigasse

VIENNA'S ENGLISH THEATRE
englishtheatre.at

This theater, founded in 1963, presents solid productions of mainstream English-language drama and comedy, given a pep by a host of visiting stars.

➕ D4 ✉ Josefsgasse 12 ☎ 402 12 600 🚇 U2 to Rathaus, U3 to Volkstheater 🚋 Trams 1, D to Parlament

Where to Eat

PRICES
Prices are approximate, based on a 3-course meal for one person.
€€€ over €40
€€ €20–€40
€ under €20

CAFÉ DRECHSLER (€€)

cafedrechsler.at

With its understatedly plain furnishings and friendly atmosphere, the original Naschmarkt café is unmissable when in the neighborhood. It has serves big breakfasts and delicous Austrian mains.

🔲 E6 ✉ Linke Wienzeile 22 ☎ 581 20 44 🕐 Sun–Thu 8am–midnight, Fri–Sat 8am–2am 🚇 U4 to Kettenbrückengasse

CAFÉ EILES (€€)

cafe-eiles.at

Situated in a mainly residential area, this is a congenial, old-fashioned Viennese coffeehouse with cozy niches.

🔲 D4 ✉ Josefstädterstrasse 2 ☎ 405 34 10 🕐 Mon–Fri 7am–10pm, Sat–Sun, hols 8am–10pm 🚇 U2 to Rathaus 🚊 Trams 1, D to Rathaus

CAFÉ LANDTMANN (€€)

landtmann.at

One of the classic Ringstrassen cafés, frequented by foreign correspondents reading international newspapers and by local ones attending the frequent press conferences held on its premises.

🔲 E4 ✉ Universitätsring 4 ☎ 24 100 100 🕐 Daily 7.30am–midnight. Live piano music Sun–Tue 8pm–11pm. Closed Sun Jul–Aug 🚊 Trams 1, D to Burgtheater

CAFÉ SCHWARZENBERG (€€)

cafe-schwarzenberg.at

This is the oldest of the elegant Ringstrassen cafés, opened in 1861 when the boulevard was still under construction. Cakes, light meals and coffees can be enjoyed here but you can also enjoy a full evening meal. There is a choice of newspapers, including foreign ones, and there are decadent touches, such as the large selection of cigars for sale. Live piano music can be enjoyed in the evenings every Thursday to Sunday.

🔲 G6 ✉ Kärntner Ring 17 ☎ 512 8998 🕐 Mon–Fri 7.30am–midnight, Sat–Sun 8.30am–midnight 🚊 Trams 2, D to Schwarzenbergplatz

CAFÉ SPERL (€€)

cafesperl.at

Established in 1880, this is one of the city's oldest and most authentic cafés. It still sports its Jugendstil fittings and even has its very own gateau—the Sperl Torte involving heaps of almonds and chocolate cream.

🔲 E6 ✉ Gumpendorferstrasse 11 ☎ 586 41 58 🕐 Mon–Sat 7am–10pm, Sun 11–8. Closed Sun Jul–Aug 🚇 U1 to Karlsplatz, U2 to MuseumsQuartier, U4 to Kettenbrückengasse

GLACIS BEISL

glacisbeisl.at

Well concealed down a flight of steps off Breite Gasse, this MuseumsQuartier Beisl does a killer goulash and its schnitzel isn't bad either. It's one of the most characterful places to eat in the neighborhood and therefore chock-a-block at mealtimes.

🔲 D5 ✉ Breite Gasse 4 ☎ 526 56 60 🚇 U2 to MuseumsQuartier

PIARISTENKELLER (€€€)

piaristenkeller.com

Crammed into the brick vaults of the Piarist monastery, this restaurant is one of the most convivial in Vienna. It is

decorated with flags, pictures as well as historic items. Don't miss the mildly Monty Pythonesque hat parade.

🔲 C4 ✉ Piaristengasse 45 ☎ 406 01 93
🕐 Daily 6pm–midnight Ⓜ U2 to Rathaus
🚋 Tram 2 to Lederergasse/Strozzigasse

RATHAUSKELLER (€€)

wiener-rathauskeller.at

In the huge neo-Gothic Rathaus (City Hall, ▷ 55), the restaurant's various rooms are decorated in Historicist style. It's big enough to escape the bus parties and the food is good.

🔲 D4 ✉ New City Hall, Rathausplatz 1/ Felderstrasse ☎ 405 12 10 🕐 Mon–Sat 11.30–3, 6–11.30 Ⓜ U2 to Rathaus 🚋 Trams 1, D to Burgtheater

RESTAURANT WIENER (€€)

restaurant-wiener.at

This is a friendly neighborhood *Beisl* (tavern), serving classic Austrian dishes like fried bread dumplings with egg, *Tafelspitz*, Wiener schnitzel and fried cheese. The local wines are good too.

🔲 C5 ✉ Hermanngasse 27A ☎ 524 52 52 🕐 Mon–Sat 4.30pm–1am, Sun to midnight. Ⓜ U3 to Neubaugasse 🚌 Bus 13A to Siebensterngasse; tram 49 to Neubaugasse

DAS SCHICK (€€€)

das-schick.at

This restaurant, located on the top floor of the Hotel Am Parkring, enjoys panoramic views over the rooftops of the city. It is a popular choice for special occasions and intimate dinner rendezvous. The menu features fusion dishes combining Austrian fare with Spanish influences.

🔲 G5 ✉ Hotel Am Parkring, Parkring 12 ☎ 514 80 417 🕐 Mon–Fri 12–3, 6–10.30, Sat–Sun 6pm–10.30pm Ⓜ U3 to Stubentor 🚋 Tram 2 to Weihburggasse

SLUKA (€€)

sluka.at

Another candidate for the title of Vienna's best patisserie, Sluka serves mouthwatering pastries and a tempting range of light lunches. Try some of the delicious petit fours or a slice of the melt-in-the-mouth Sachertorte. On a sunny day the outside terrace is perfect for people-watching while enjoying a leisurely coffee.

🔲 D4 ✉ Rathausplatz 8 ☎ 512 49 63 500 🕐 Mon–Sat 8.30–8, Sun 10–6 🚋 Trams 1, D to Rathaus

ZU EBENER ERDE UND ERSTER STOCK (€€)

zu-ebener-erde-und-erster-stock.at

The Spittelberg area has many good eateries but this is the best, serving Viennese cooking with a light touch and with much attention to seasonal specialties like asparagus. There's also a very good wine list. The smarter restaurant part is upstairs, while the lower part is less pretentious; there is a good atmosphere in both areas. The three-course set menu is great budget option.

🔲 D5 ✉ Burggasse 13 ☎ 523 62 54 🕐 Mon–Fri 12–10 Ⓜ U2, U3 to Volkstheater

THE *BEISL*

Most restaurants offering genuine Viennese cooking are carrying on the *Beisl* tradition: Honest food, cooked and served in unpretentious surroundings. The word is of Yiddish origin (in the past, tavern keepers were often Jewish). Some *Beisls* have transformed into expensive restaurants, but many hold to tradition and keep their prices fair. Typical dishes include *Tafelspitz* (boiled beef), *Zwiebelrostbraten* (beefsteak with crispy onions) and *Beuschel* (chopped lung in sauce). Liver is also popular.

GVSTAV KLIMT

Around Alsergrund

Alsergrund is a residential area dotted with palaces, churches and other places of interest, notably Sigmund Freud's home, where he lived for 47 years.

Top 25

Freud Haus	**68**
Palais Liechtenstein	**70**
More to See	**71**
Walk	**72**
Shopping	**73**
Entertainment and Nightlife	**74**
Where to Eat	**75**

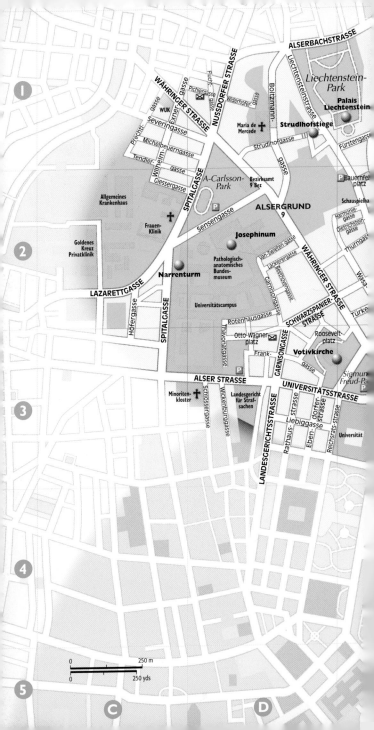

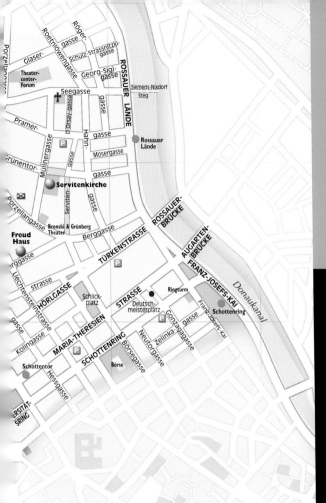

Porzellangasse

Röger-
gasse

Roethlöwengasse

Glaser-
gasse

Schulz-Strassnitzki-
gasse

Georg-Sigl-
gasse

ROSSAUER LÄNDE

Theater-
center-
Forum

Seegasse

Siemens-Nixdorf
Steg

Pramer-

D'Orsav-gasse

Hann-

gasse

gasse

Rossauer
Lände

Grünentor-

Müllnergasse

Mosergasse

gasse

gasse

Servitenkirche

Porzellangasse

Serviten-

gasse

Bronski & Grünberg
Theater

Berggasse

ROSSAUER-
BRÜCKE

Freud
Haus

erggasse

TÜRKENSTRASSE

AUGARTEN-
BRÜCKE

FRANZ-JOSEFS-KAI

Liechtensteinstrasse

strasse

HÖRLGASSE

Schlick-
platz

STRASSE

Ringturm

Donaukanal

gasse

Kolingasse

MARIA-THERESIEN

Deutsch-
meisterplatz

Gonzagagasse

Franz-Josefs-Kai

Schottenring

SCHOTTENRING

Zelinka-

gasse

Schottentor

Hessgasse

Börsegasse

Neutorgasse

Börse

ERSITÄT-
SRING

E   F

Freud Haus

HIGHLIGHTS

● Freud's hat and cane
hanging in the entrance hall
● Library
● Research Center
● Freud's antiques—he
owned over 3,000

Some of the 20th century's most influential ideas stemmed from the tenant of No. 5, Berggasse 19, and it is interesting to see the place where his work began.

Sigmund Freud Recognized as the founder of modern psychoanalysis, Freud (1856–1939) was nonetheless typically Viennese, playing *tarock* (a card game still popular with the older generation), visiting Café Landtmann (▷ 62) and taking a daily constitutional along the entire length of the Ringstrasse. Most of his possessions are held in London, where he fled to escape Nazi persecution in 1938 (a year before his death). However, his youngest daughter, Anna, donated some items for display here, and his waiting room and the entrance hall

Clockwise from left: Detail from a decorative window; a caricature and some of Freud's personal effects; inside Freud's apartment; outside the Freud Haus

appear as they would have done while he lived and worked in the apartment for almost half a century.

Theories Freud's most controversial theory was that infantile sexual impulses were at the root of adult neuroses. Adler and Jung—the other famous early psychoanalysts—parted company with him over this. However, many now-mainstream concepts started with Freud—for example, division of the personality into id and ego, and the ideas of sublimation and the Oedipus complex. Although many academics still accept Freud's theories, his critics believe that he doctored his evidence. The Viennese writer Karl Kraus, a contemporary of Freud's, remarked: "Psychoanalysis is the disease of which it purports to be the cure."

THE BASICS

freud-museum.at

🞤 E2

✉ Berggasse 19

☎ 319 15 96

🕑 Daily 10–6

🚇 U2 to Schottentor

🚌 Tram D to Schlickgasse

♿ None

🎟 Moderate

Palais Liechtenstein

Archway (left) in front of the Palais Liechtenstein (right)

THE BASICS

palaisliechtenstein.com

⊞ E1

✉ Fürstengasse 1

☎ 319 57 67 153

🕐 Admission by guided tour only: Fri 3–4

🚇 U4 to Rossauer Lände

🚌 Bus 40A; tram D to Bauernfeldplatz

♿ Good

💲 Expensive

❓ Tours require prebooking, either by phone or online

HIGHLIGHTS

● Badminton Cabinet, bought at auction in 2004 for a record-breaking 227 million euros

● Large series of Rubens paintings

● Baroque garden, reconstructed from old prints

This superbly renovated palace displays a major part of the artistic estate of the celebrated Liechtenstein family, rulers of the principality of the same name.

The Liechtensteins One of the oldest noble families of Europe, the Liechtensteins were first mentioned in 1136. They derive their name from Liechtenstein Castle, a stone's throw from Vienna. Elevated to princes in 1608, in 1719 they acquired their own sovereign state.

Garden Palace When Hitler invaded Austria in 1938, the Prince of Liechtenstein retreated to his own pocket-handkerchief state, taking his famous art collection with him. In 2004, part of that collection was returned to the family's Garden Palace (summer palace) in Vienna. A state-of-the-art gallery was created to make viewing as pleasurable and informal as possible, so you feel you are enjoying the pictures as the Liechtensteins would themselves have done.

The collection No attempt has been made to cram the rooms with art, and the clear aim is to maximize the viewer's pleasure; if you want to know more there is a helpful audio guide. Visitors should note that opening hours are limited and prebooking is required. As well as masterpieces, ranging from Gothic to fin de siècle, the museum contains the Badminton Cabinet, which was originally made for an ancestor of the Duke of Beaufort by Florentine craftsmen in 1732.

More to See

JOSEPHINUM

josephinum.ac.at

Aspiring military surgeons pored over lifelike anatomical wax models here, preparing for a career on the battlefields of the Empire. The building now houses the Museum of Medical History.

➕ D2 ✉ Währinger Strasse 25 ☎ 401 60 26 000 🕐 Museum of Medical History: Mon–Thu 9–4 🚋 Trams 37, 38, 40, 41, 42 to Sensengasse 🎟 Inexpensive ❓ Guided tour in English Sat at 11am

NARRENTURM

The Narrenturm was used as an asylum until 1866; subsequently it housed a store and provided living quarters for medical staff. It is now the Museum for Pathology and Anatomy, and contains a large collection of medical curiosities.

➕ C2 ✉ Corner of Sensengasse and Spitalgasse (up a zigzagging path) ☎ 406 86 722 🕐 Wed 10am–6pm, Thu & Sat 10am–1pm 🚇 U2 to Schottentor 🚋 Tram 5 to Lazarettgasse; 43, 44 to Lange Gasse 🎟 Inexpensive ♿ None

An exhibit in the Josephinum

SERVITENKIRCHE

The fine cupola of the 17th-century Servite Church served as a prototype for other baroque churches in the city. A chapel inside is dedicated to the Servite St. Peregrine, who is invoked for healing lameness. The saint was a great benefactor of the poor, and special bread rolls are still distributed in the Servitengassse during the two-day St. Peregrine's fair in May.

➕ E2 ✉ Servitengasse 9 ☎ 317 61 950 🕐 Daily 8–7 🚇 U4 to Rossauer Lände 🚋 Tram D to Schlickgasse ♿ Two steps 🎟 Free

STRUDLHOFSTIEGE

This outdoor, graceful art nouveau stairway with lanterns and wells was designed in 1910 by Theodor Jäger. The steps are especially attractive at night when lit by the stairway lanterns.

➕ D1 ✉ Strudlhofgasse 🚇 U4 to Rossauer Lände 🚋 Tram D to Bauernfeldplatz

VOTIVKIRCHE

This huge neo-Gothic church was built to commemorate Emperor Franz Josef's escape from an assassination attempt in 1853. Its chapels are dedicated to Austrian regiments. Look for the Renaissance sarcophagus of Count Salm, defender of Vienna in the Turkish siege of 1529.

➕ D3 ✉ Rooseveltplatz 8 ☎ 406 11 920 🕐 Tue–Fri 4–6, Sat–Sun 9–1 🚇 U2 to Schottentor 🚋 Trams 1, 2 to Schottentor ♿ Several steps 🎟 Church free; museum inexpensive ❓ Holy Mass in English Sun at 11

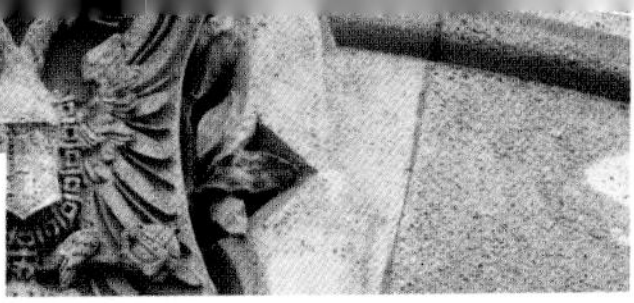

Alsergrund Stroll

This is an attractive residential area of Vienna, dotted with a variety of churches, palaces and museums.

DISTANCE: 2.5 miles (4km) **ALLOW:** 2 hours without visits

START

SCHOTTENTOR
E3 🚇 U2 to Schottentor
🚌 Trams 1, 2

END

SCHOTTENTOR

❶ Approach the overblown neo-Gothic Votivkirche (▷ 71) by walking through the Sigmund Freud Park opposite the Schottentor tram junction.

❷ On leaving the church, turn northeast onto Währinger Strasse. Continue to the next traffic lights, then take a right down Berggasse to the Freud Museum (▷ 68).

❸ Continue along Berggasse until the crossroads, then follow the lively Servitengasse to the Servitenkirche (▷ 71). You can enjoy good local fare at the Servitenwirt (▷ 75).

❹ From the Servitenkirche turn left and follow Grünentorgasse to the end and turn right on Porzellangasse. Just a few steps from here turn left to find the Palais Liechtenstein (▷ 70).

❺ On leaving the palace courtyard, take two right turns.

❻ Cross Liechtensteinstrasse and climb the art nouveau steps of Strudlhofstiege (▷ 71). Take Boltzmanngasse to the left and cross Währinger Strasse for the Josephinum (Museum of Medical History, ▷ 71).

❼ From the Josephinum, take two right turns for Van-Swieten-Gasse. Once inside the university campus, follow the Leopold-Bauer-Weg to the Narrenturm (▷ 71), screened by trees to your right. Retrace Leopold-Bauer-Weg and continue through Courtyard 7 to Courtyard 1.

❽ Refreshment is available at several inexpensive restaurants here. After leaving the campus by the exit to your left, return to Schottentor on foot or one stop on the tram.

Shopping

DEMMERS TEEHAUS

tee.at

The genuine Chinese or Indian teas available here will please those who are dispirited by the tea bag and hot water that is sold as "tea" in cafés and restaurants of the notoriously coffee-bound Vienna. Not surprisingly, the founder and owner Andrew Demmer was born in London and returned with his parents from exile after World War II. There's an amazing selection of tea-related gifts and products that make ideal souvenirs. There is also a tea salon upstairs where you can choose from 250 types of tea.

➕ E3 ✉ Mölkerbastei 5 ☎ 533 59 95 🕐 Sep–Jun Mon–Fri 9–6, Sat 9.30–1.30. Tearoom Mon–Fri 10–6 🚇 U2 to Schottentor 🚌 Buses 1A, 3A to Schottentor; trams 1, 2, D to Schottentor

FÜRNIS MÄDCHEN UND BUBEN

fuernis.com

This shop began by importing and selling wooden toys from other countries and factories, but the owners felt that something was missing and decided to design toys themselves. Their soft, friendly dolls and animals are now exported to many countries. Other items for sale include sleeping bags, bookmarks—and much more.

➕ E2 ✉ Servitengasse 4a ☎ 968 62 33 🕐 Mon–Fri 9.30–6.30, Sat 9.30–2 🚇 U4 to Rossauer Lände 🚌 Tram D to Schlickgasse

PALAIS FERSTEL

palaisevents.at

The grand Palais Ferstel teleports you back to a more glamorous retail era with classy emporia (jewelry, pricey chocolate, upscale delicatessen) filling the arches of this neo-Renaissance palace. It's odd in being named for its architect, Heinrich von Ferstel,

rather than its mid-19th-century aristocratic owner.

➕ E3 ✉ Strauchgasse 4 🚇 U3 to Herrengasse

TOSTMANN TRACHTEN

tostmann.at

This is the place to go for clothing with a traditional *Tracht* look, for men, women and children. Choose between unobtrusive fashion or the full Monty. Every federal province of Austria has its own version of *Tracht*.

➕ E3 ✉ Schottengasse 3A (corner to Mölkerbastei stairs) ☎ 533 53 31 🕐 Mon–Fri 10–7, Sat 10–6 🚇 U2 to Schottentor 🚌 Buses 1A, 3A to Schottentor; trams 1, 2, D to Schottentor

UNGER UND KLEIN

ungerundklein.at

The best selection of wines from Lower Austria, Styria and Burgenland and the interior by Eichinger oder Knechtl make the detour worth it. They also have a daily wine offer designed to match the weather and your (or their) mood which can be enjoyed with delicous antipasti.

➕ F3 ✉ Gölsdorfgasse 2 ☎ 532 13 23 🕐 Mon–Fri 5–10, Sat 5–midnight 🚇 U1, U4 to Schwedenplatz

XOCOLAT MANUFAKTUR

This fine chocolate shop was opened under the guidance of top chef Christian Petz (who also runs the popular Holy-Moly! restaurant, ▷ 45). Chocolate bars and truffles are made on the premises—you can watch the chocolatiers as they work. There's also another branch in the shopping arcade at Freyung 2, Palais Ferstel.

➕ E2 ✉ Servitengasse 5 ☎ 310 00 20 🕐 Mon–Fri 10–6, Sat 10–1 🚇 U4 to Rossauer Lände 🚌 Tram D to Schlickgasse

Entertainment and Nightlife

OPEN HOUSE THEATRE COMPANY

openhousetheatre.at

This is the successor to the erstwhile Vienna International Theatre. The Open House Theatre Company aims to bring high-level English-language theater to both the English-language community and locals who like to practice their English. Note that while the company's offices are near Alsergrund, performances take place in theaters all over the city. Check online for performances during your visit and you can buy tickets over the phone or online.

🔲 Off map at D1 ⊠ Döblinger Hauptstrasse 33A/20 ☎ 680 225 12 90 🕙 Hours vary according to performance

PFARRKIRCHE LICHTENTAL

schubertkirche.at

Composer Franz Schubert was the greatest son of the Lichtental parish. The church where he was baptized, received his first exposure to music and where some of his great masses were first performed has hardly changed from his time. There are Schubert Days in late November and regular organ recitals at other times of the year.

🔲 Off map at D1 ⊠ Marktgasse 40/ Lichtentalergasse ☎ 315 26 46 🚇 U4 to Friedensbrücke 🚋 Tram D to Althanstrasse

SUMMER STAGE

summerstage.at

From May to September Vienna's popular Summer Stage along the Alsergrund Danube Canal is a magnet for young people. Viennese food and international fare is on offer, together with concerts and lectures, exhibitions, sporting facilities—and even a doggy watering hole with all canine comforts. A great option for a casual and fun night.

🔲 F1/2 ⊠ Rossauer Lände south of Mosergasse ☎ 315 52 02 🕙 May–Sep daily 5pm–1am, Sun 3pm–1am 🚇 U4 to Rossauer Lände

VOLKSOPER

volksoper.at

Even though it's in the uncongenial area of the *Gürtel* (Ring Road), the Volksoper is no poor relation of the Staatsoper. For visitors this is the best place to enjoy the operettas and some German operas hardly performed in the English-speaking world. For the locals it's a good place to see imported musicals and foreign-language operas in German. There are also ballet and solo performances. The Volksoper may not have the budget to engage internationally acclaimed opera stars but, like the English National Opera or the New York City Opera, it contributes something uniquely democratic to the city's musical scene.

🔲 C1 ⊠ Währinger Strasse 78 ☎ 51 444 36 70 🚇 U6 to Währinger Strasse-Volksoper 🚌 Bus 40A; trams 40, 41, 42 to Währinger Strasse-Volksoper

WUK

wuk.at

An arts area with a café and restaurant, also performance art, dance and DJ nights. Situated in a rundown former locomotive factory, the WUK has developed into one of Europe's largest and hottest art scenes, hosting 130 groups. The heart of Vienna's alternative culture, it focuses both on international trends and local innovations.

🔲 C1 ⊠ Währinger Strasse 59 ☎ 401 210 🕙 Mon–Fri 9–8, Sat–Sun 3–8. Hours vary according to events 🚇 U6 to Währinger Strasse-Volksoper 🚋 Trams 40, 41, 42 to Währinger Strasse-Volksoper

Where to Eat

PRICES

Prices are approximate, based on a 3-course meal for one person.

€€€   over €40
€€   €20–€40
€   under €20

BERG (€€)

This long-established café and restaurant for the gay community sits adjacent to the Löwenherz (Lionheart) bookshop with its gay and feminist literature. Berg has a cool vibe in a modern setting; it's well known for its brunch (daily 10–3) and constantly changing menu.

🔛 E2 ✉ Berggasse 8/ Wasagasse ☎ 319 57 20 🕒 Tue–Sat 10am–11pm, Sun 10–3 🚇 U2 to Schottentor 🚊 Trams 37, 38, 40, 41 to Schwarzspanierstrasse

ETHIOPIAN RESTAURANT (€€)

ethiopianrestaurant.at

Main dishes are served in a traditional style, with meats, spicy vegetables and condiments all piled atop a giant flattened piece of Ethiopian bread called *injera*. On Fridays and Saturdays they hold an Ethiopian coffee ceremony at 8.30pm.

🔛 D2 ✉ Währinger Strasse 15 ☎ 40 20 726 🕒 Tue–Sat 11–11, Sun 3–11 🚇 U2 to Schottentor 🚊 Trams 37, 38, 40, 41 to Schwarzspanierstrasse

PORZELLAN (€€)

porzellan-lounge.at

This contemporary restaurant and bar serves Austrian and international cuisine in a bright, modern setting. The place now opens too late to enjoy the *Grosses Erwachen* (Great Awakening) breakfast, so pop in at lunchtime for the inexpensive midday menu.

🔛 E2 ✉ Servitengasse 2 ☎ 315 63 63 🕒 Mon–Fri 10am–midnight, Sat–Sun 9am–midnight 🚇 U2 to Schottentor 🚊 Tram D to Schlickgasse

RAGUSA (€€€)

ragusa.at

Ragusa is the Italian name for Dubrovnik and it's the seafood of the Adriatic, air-freighted in daily from the Dalmatian coast, that you'll discover on the menu here. There's a wide range of wines from Croatia as well as a inexpensive lunch menu.

🔛 E2 ✉ Berggasse 15 ☎ 317 15 77 🕒 Mon–Fri 11.30–2, 6–10, Sat 6pm–10pm 🚇 U2 to Schottentor 🚊 Trams 37, 38, 40, 41 to Schwarzspanierstrasse

ROTH (€€)

kremslehnerhotels.at

A stylish restaurant offering Viennese classics such as *Tafelspitz* (boiled beef) and *Zwiebelrostbraten* (beef steak with crispy onions). It's under the same management as the Hotel Regina—you can peek from the arcade into the latter's majestic former dining room.

🔛 E3 ✉ Währinger Strasse 1/Rooseveltplatz ☎ 402 79 95 🕒 Daily 11–12 🚇 U2 to Schottentor 🚊 Trams 37, 38, 40, 41, 42, 43, 44 to Schottentor

SERVITENWIRT (€€)

servitenwirt.at

Servitenwirt offers a full range of classic Viennese dishes, served in an unpretentious, traditional setting. They also sell their own wine from Lower Austria. In the summer, there's a pleasant terrace area to dine in.

🔛 E2 ✉ Servitengasse 7, beside Servite Church ☎ 315 23 87 🕒 Daily 11–11 🚇 U4 to Rossauer Lände 🚊 Tram D to Schlickgasse ❓ Summer garden

Around Landstrasse, Wieden

This area features two of Europe's greatest baroque buildings: The Belvedere Palace and Karlskirche. Both palace and church, with their monumental architecture, have justly made the city renowned for its splendid late-flowering of the style.

Top 25

Heeresgeschichtliches Museum **80**

Karlskirche **81**

Schloss Belvedere **82**

Wien Museum **84**

More to See **85**

Walk **86**

Shopping **87**

Entertainment and Nightlife **88**

Where to Eat **89**

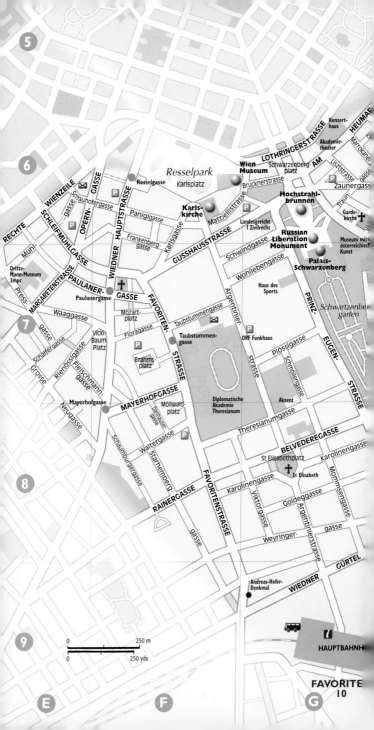

5

6

7

8

9

Konzert-
haus
Akademie-
theater
LOTHRINGERSTRASSE
Marrokkan

Resselpark
Karlsplatz

**Wien
Museum**

Schwarzenberg-
platz

AM

Lizststrasse

Zaunergasse

P

Traun-

Garde-
kirche

Museum mit
österreichisch
Kunst

Bruckner-
strasse

**Hochstrahl-
brunnen**

Resselgasse

**Karls-
kirche**

Mattiellistrasse

GUSSHAUSSTRASSE

Panigigasse

Landesgericht
f Zivilrecht

**Russian
Liberation
Monument**

WIENZEILE

GASSE

OPERN-

WIEDNER HAUPTSTRASSE

Schauhofergasse

gasse

P

**Palais-
Schwarzenberg**

PRINZ-

*Schwartzenber
garten*

Karlsgasse

Frankenber-
gasse

Schwindgasse

Wohllebengasse

SCHLEIFMÜHLGASSE

RECHTE

Mühl-

press.-

Dritte-
Mann-Museum
3mpc

PAULANER-

GASSE

Haus des
Sports

EUGEN-

MARGARETENSTRASSE

Paulanergasse

Taubstummengasse

Argentinier-

ORF Funkhaus

STRASSE

Waaggasse

Mozart-
platz

Floragasse

Taubstummen-
gasse

Plösslgasse

gasse

Schäffergasse

Vlckl-
Baum
Platz

P

Brahms-
platz

strasse

Schmöllergasse

Grosse

Rienösslgasse

Fleischmann-
gasse

FAVORITEN-

Mayerhofgasse

MAYERHOFGASSE

Möllwald-
platz

Diplomatische
Akademie
Theresianum

Akzent

Neulgasse

damasse-
gasse

Theresianumgasse

BELVEDEREGASSE

Waltergasse

Schaumburgergasse

STRASSE

St Elisabethplatz

Karolinengasse

Mommsengasse

8

Starhembergasse

St Elisabeth

Karolinengasse

Viktorgasse

Goldeggasse

Argentinierstrasse

RAINERGASSE

FAVORITENSTRASSE

gasse

Weyringergasse

WIEDNER

GÜRTEL

Andreas-Hofer-
Denkmal

i

HAUPTBAHNH

0 _____ 250 m
0 _____ 250 yds

9

**FAVORITE
10**

E   F   G

R-Sallinger-platz

Bayerngasse

Grimmelshausen-

Gottfried-Keller-gasse

Salesianer-gasse

Neuling-

gasse

Strasse

oh-

gasse

Russische Kirche ✝

Linke Bahngasse

Jaurès- ✝

gasse

Metternichgasse

Reisner

Rechte Bahngasse

Ungargasse

Stanislausgasse

Unteres Belvedere

RENNWEG

✝

P

✝

Rennweg

Salesianerinnen-kloster

Schützen-

gasse

vederegarten

Praetorius-gasse

P

Magazin-gasse

Mechelgasse

Fasanplatz

RENNWEG

Aspangstrasse

Obere

Bahngasse

Joseph-Schmidt-platz

Schloss Belvedere

Botanischer Garten der Universität

Jacquingasse

Gerlgasse

Kellgasse

Göschlgasse

Fasangasse

Hegergasse

gasse

Platz der Opfer der Deportation

Kölblgasse

Hohlweggasse

Khunngasse

✝

Kärchergasse

Adolf-Blamauer-Gasse

Mohs-

gasse

Kleist-

gasse

Alpengarten

Trubelgasse

LANDSTRASSER

GÜRTEL

Heinrich-Drimmel-platz

Quartier Belvedere

Schweizer Gartenstrasse

Heeresmuseumstrasse

Schweizergarten

Kelsenstrasse

ARSENALSTRASSE

Belvedere 21

Ghegastrasse

Heeresgeschichtliches Museum

H

J

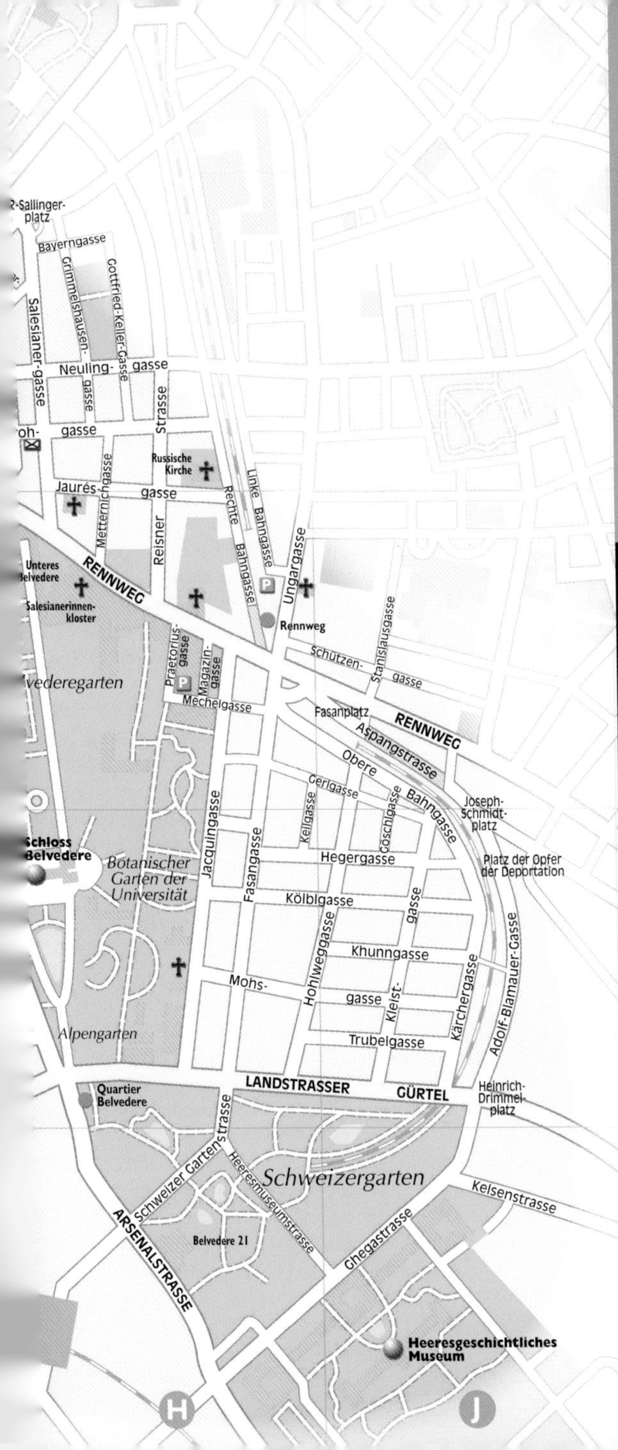

Heeresgeschichtliches Museum

The museum's exterior (left); the car in which the Archduke was killed (right)

THE BASICS

hgm.at

➕ J9

✉ Arsenal Objekt 1

☎ 795 610

🕐 Daily 9–5

🍴 Café

🚌 Bus 13A to Quartier Belvedere; trams O, D, 18 to Quartier Belvedere

🚉 Schnellbahn to Quartier Belvedere; U1 to Südtirolerplatz/ Hauptbahnhof

♿ Good

💰 Moderate; free first Sun of month

❓ Audio guide

HIGHLIGHTS

● Ornate Byzantine facade
Ground floor
● *To the Unknown Soldier* (1916), Albin Egger Lienz
● Car in which Archduke Franz Ferdinand was assassinated
● Bloodstained uniform of Archduke Franz Ferdinand
● Tank park

Housed in Vienna's gigantic pseudo-Byzantine, red-brick Arsenal, the unmissable Museum of Military History contains some intriguing exhibits that provide an insight into four centuries of Austria's imperial history and covers the period from the Thirty Years' War to WWII.

Riot-proof After the revolution of 1848, during which Am Hof, the old town armory, was plundered, leading Ringstrassen architects were commissioned to design a riot-proof arms factory and depot. This state-of-the-art complex was built with eight fortress-like barracks along its perimeter; by 1854 the facilities it enclosed were like those of an entire city within a city. The task of constructing it created jobs at a time of social unrest and unemployment. After World War II, some of the complex was rebuilt, and part is now occupied by state-owned drama workshops and a telecommunications facility, as well as the Museum of Military History.

Collection Themed sections include the Thirty Years' War (1618–48), the Napoleonic Wars and the Austrian Navy (in existence until 1918). Particularly gruesome is the bloodstained tunic Archduke Franz Ferdinand, heir to the Habsburg throne, was wearing when he was assassinated in June 1914—an event that triggered the start of World War I. The museum also includes a display on "Republic and Dictatorship," which covers the period from the fall of the Habsburg Empire up to 1945.

St. Charles's Church is awash with fine baroque detailing

Karlskirche

St. Charles's Church is one of Europe's finest baroque buildings. The symbolism in the two exotic columns at the front, fashioned on Trajan's Column in Rome, illustrates Habsburg secular power and spiritual legitimacy.

Origins In 1713 Vienna was hit by the last of many plagues; Emperor Charles VI vowed to dedicate a church to St. Charles Borromeo, who cared for the people during the 1576 Milan plague. Begun in 1716, it is the masterpiece of Johann Bernhard Fischer von Erlach, who died in 1723, leaving his son, Joseph Emanuel, to complete it in 1739.

Paean in stone The two columns at the front symbolize the Pillars of Hercules in the Mediterranean, a reference to the Spanish realm (by then lost) of the other Habsburg line. Their spiraling friezes show the life of Charles Borromeo. The columns are also emblems of the Emperor's motto, "*Constantia et fortitudine*" (Through perseverance and bravery). The russet, gold and white interior creates a harmonious tranquility.

Paintings Austrian and Central European baroque is characterized by bright frescoes with spiritual motifs, and the Karlskirche houses Johann Michael Rottmayr's wonderful painting, soaring into the cupola, shows the *Apotheosis of Charles Borromeo*. Among the other works is *Assumption of the Virgin* by Sebastiano Ricci.

THE BASICS

karlskirche.at

➕ F6

✉ Karlsplatz

☎ 504 61 87

🕐 Mon–Sat 9–6, Sun 12–7

🚇 U1, U2, U4 to Karlsplatz

🚌 Bus 4A to Karlsplatz; trams 1, 62 to Karlsplatz

♿ Good

💰 Moderate

❓ Audio guide

HIGHLIGHTS

● *Apotheosis of Charles Borromeo*, J. M. Rottmayr
● *Christ and the Centurion*, Daniel Gran
● *The Healing of the Man with the Palsy*, Giovanni Pellegrini
● Carved pulpit with rocaille and floral decoration

TIP

● It is possible to access the cupola to view the ceiling fresco close up and get a panoramic view of the city.

Schloss Belvedere

HIGHLIGHTS

Lower Belvedere
● Balthasar Permoser's statue of Prince Eugene
Upper Belvedere
● Sala Terrena with Hercules figures
● *The Kiss*, Gustav Klimt
● *Death and the Maiden*, Egon Schiele

TIP

● Visit the Botanical Garden and fragrant Alpine Garden adjacent to the gardens south of the Upper Belvedere.

After St. Stephen's Cathedral (▷ 31), the Belvedere Palace complex is Vienna's most important landmark. Between the Upper Belvedere in the south and the Lower Belvedere in the south stretch Versailles-style gardens like no others in central Europe.

Origins Lukas von Hildebrandt constructed the Lower Belvedere (Unteres Belvedere) between 1714 and 1716. The magnificent Upper Belvedere (Oberes Belvedere), designed to house Prince Eugene's fabulous art collection, appeared between 1721 and 1723.

Palace in history Emperor Josef II installed the Imperial Picture Gallery in the Upper Belvedere. Franz Ferdinand, the heir to the throne, lived

Clockwise from far left: Klimt's Kiss is one of the popular pieces on display, the impressive Upper Belvedere; a sweeping view of the palace's grounds

here from 1899 until his assassination in 1914. In 1955 the Austrian State Treaty ending the Allied occupation was signed in the Marble Hall.

Museums The entrance to the Belvedere galleries is at the Lower Belvedere, which contains Prince Eugene's rooms, including the Golden Salon. The adjacent Orangery has been adapted for special exhibitions and the former stables display minor works of medieval art. Major medieval works and baroque paintings are now concentrated in the Upper Belvedere. However the main attraction remains the collection of masterpieces by Klimt, Schiele and Kokoschka, together with international art from the 19th century and later. Post-1945 art and the Fritz Wotruba collection are exhibited at 21er Haus in nearby Schweizergarten.

THE BASICS

belvedere.at

➕ H8

✉ Lower Belvedere: Rennweg 6; Upper Belvedere: Prinz-Eugen-Strasse 27

☎ 79 557 134 (tour information and booking)

🕐 Collections: Daily 10–6 (Wed until 9). Stables: 10–noon. Shorter hours on 1 Jan, 24, 31 Dec. Alpine Garden: Apr–Jul 10–6

🍴 Café in Upper Belvedere

🚃 Tram 71 (Lower Belvedere), 0, 18 (Upper Belvedere), D (Upper and Lower belvederes)

💰 Expensive

♿ Good

❓ Audio guide

Wien Museum

TOP 25

Entrance to the Wien Museum (left); Lady in a Yellow Dress by Max Kurzweil (right)

THE BASICS

wienmuseum.at

➕ F6

✉ Karlsplatz

☎ 505 87 47

🕐 Tue–Sun 10–6.

🍽 Café

Ⓤ U1, U2, U4 to Karlsplatz

♿ Good

💰 Moderate. Permanent exhibition free on first Sun of month

HIGHLIGHTS

● Eduard Fischer's maquette of the old town, 1854
● Franz Xaver Messerschmidt's grotesque busts
● *Stephansplatz* (1834), Rudolf von Alt
● Reconstructed apartment of playwright Franz Grillparzer
● Reconstructed sitting room in architect Adolf Loos's house
● *Anna Moll, Writing*, Carl Moll

Although housed in a drab 1950s-style building, the Viennese History Museum is one of Europe's best city museums, and its well-displayed contents bring the Viennese past vividly to life.

Origins The characterless design of the structure—its banality made more striking by its juxtaposition with the baroque architecture of St. Charles's Church next door—aroused much anger among Viennese patriots, although it had its defenders.

Museum collection Vienna's history, topography, art and culture are explored in the many works of art and architectural relics, and in the early city plans, the reconstructions of interiors like Adolf Loos's living room and Franz Grillparzer's Biedermeier apartment, and in the beautifully made period models of the city.

Sweeping view The ground floor spans pre-history (Hallstatt culture) up to and including medieval times. On the first floor are exhibits of the baroque period and Enlightenment. The material relating to the time of the Turkish siege of Vienna (weapons and a portrait of Turkish commander Kara Mustafa) is of particular interest.

Other Sites The Vienna Museum isn't just about the Karlsplatz building. The museum looks after 21 other sites across Vienna, check online for more details.

More to See

HOCHSTRAHLBRUNNEN

In 1873, a huge fountain was built at the southern end of Schwarzenbergplatz in front of Schwarzenberg Palace to mark the opening of Vienna's first water supply from the Alpine peaks (*Hochquellenleitung*). It brought fresh water to the city from 56 miles (90km) away. The fountain is illuminated at night.

➕ G6 ✉ Schwarzenbergplatz 🚊 Trams D to Gusshausstrasse, 71 to Am Heumarkt

PALAIS-SCHWARZENBERG

In 1716, Prince Schwarzenberg bought an unfinished palace by Lukas von Hildebrandt and then commissioned Johann Bernhard Fischer von Erlach, and later his son Joseph Emanuel, to complete the structure, which is still owned by the family. The grand sweep up to the portico was conceived by the younger Fischer, who also installed Vienna's first steam-driven motor to pump water for the fountains. The Schwarzenbergs' neighbor and rival, Prince Eugene of Savoy, had to postpone his great Schloss Belvedere project (▷ 82–83) until he had persuaded the Schwarzenbergs to sell a vital piece of adjacent land.

➕ G7 ✉ Schwarzenbergplatz 9 🚫 No access to palace and garden 🚊 Tram D to Gusshausstrasse

RUSSIAN LIBERATION MONUMENT

Just behind the Hochstrahlbrunnen, this massive memorial to the Soviet Red Army recalls the period just after World War II when Vienna was divided into four occupation zones, each controlled by one of the Allied powers (Britain, France, the US and the Soviet Union). The monument, a white marble colonnade encircling a large statue of a Red Army soldier, dates from 1945 and recalls the 17,000 Red Army soldiers who fell in the battle for Vienna in April that year.

➕ G6 ✉ Schwarzenbergplatz 🚊 Trams D to Gusshausstrasse, 71 to Am Heumarkt

Hochstrahlbrunnen

Baroque at its Best

Karlskirche and the Belvedere Palace, with its gardens and fine collection of Secessionist art, are the highlights of this walk.

DISTANCE: 2.5 miles (4km) **ALLOW:** 2 hours without visits

START

KARLSPLATZ
F6 U1, U2, U4 to Karlsplatz

❶ From the underground passage connecting the Opera and Karlsplatz, take the Resselpark exit to the south. On your left you will see the Karlsplatz pavilions designed by Otto Wagner, while ahead rises Karlskirche (▷ 81).

❷ On leaving the church, turn south into Argentinierstrasse. At the second crossroads turn left and approach Schwarzenbergplatz through Gusshausstrasse.

❸ Cross Prinz-Eugen-Strasse to the Hochstrahlbrunnen (▷ 85) and the Russian Liberation Monument (▷ 85). Bear right into Rennweg.

❹ Then continue up Rennweg to the entrance of the Belvedere Palace (▷ 82–83) and museums. Having viewed the Lower Belvedere, walk up the sloping gardens to the Upper Belvedere.

END

HAUPTBAHNHOF
H9 U1 to Südtirolerplatz/
Hauptbahnhof

❽ On leaving the museum through the main gate, turn left into Ghegastrasse and then right into Arsenalstrasse.

❼ Take the path to the left of the ornamental pool and continue along the promenade. After refreshment in the Schweizergarten restaurant, head up Heeresmuseum Strasse to visit the Heeresgeschichtliches Museum (▷ 80).

❻ On leaving the Belvedere, bear right round the building and head for the Alpine Garden to your left. After visiting the garden, retrace your steps through the Belvedere's southern garden as far as the Gürtel (Ring Road), which you cross to reach the Schweizergarten.

❺ Visit the Upper Belvedere, with its collections of art, and enjoy the view of Vienna from the upper windows.

Shopping

ALOIS FRIMMEL

knopfkoenig.at

This shop, founded in 1884, sells only buttons. Maybe the "old king of buttons" has precisely the one you have been trying to find for years.

🏠 F7 ✉ Zum alten Knopfkönig, Wiedner Hauptstrasse 34 ✉ 587 92 68 🕐 Mon–Wed 10–4.45, 5.15–6, Fri 10–3.45, 4.15–6, Sat 10–1 🚋 Tram 62 to Paulanergasse

BAHNHOFCITY

hauptbahnhofcity.wien

With the opening of the new main train station at the end of 2014 came the addition of the city's newest and one of its largest shopping malls. The Bahnhofcity shopping center has some 90 stores spread out over 215,300sq ft (20,000sq m) of floor space. Stores include major clothing, design and electronics outlets. In addition, there is a branch of the city tourist office, as well as banks, restaurants and places to pick up food or drink for the train journey.

🏠 H9 ✉ Wien Hauptbahnhof, Am Hauptbahnhof 1 ☎ 051 717 🕐 Daily 9–9 🚇 U1 to Südtirolerplatz/Hauptbahnhof

EDI-BÄR

Margit Edinger sells and restores teddy bears, as well as other soft toys. There are also home-made glass bracelets and other jewelry, and typically Viennese petit-point bags.

🏠 J5 ✉ Landstrasser Hauptstrasse 28 ☎ 710 25 84 🕐 Tue–Fri 10–1, 2–6, Sat 10–1 🚇 U3 Rochusgasse 🚋 Tram O to Sechskrügelgasse

FLO VINTAGE

flovintage.com

The vintage craze long since arrived in the Austrian capital and this lovely boutique has a wonderfully curated selection of yesteryear clothing. They stock anything from 1880 to 1980, meaning lots of stylish pieces from before the days of mass production. The store does only stock women's clothing though.

🏠 E6 ✉ Schleifmühlgasse 15 ✉ 586 07 73 🕐 Mon–Fri 10–6.30, Sat 10–3.30 🚇 U4 to Kettenbrückengasse

MARIOL

mariol.info

This boutique caters for curvier women who still love their fashion, and sells unique and interesting pieces. It's a place that sells personal style as much as clothes.

🏠 J5 ✉ Landstrasser Hauptstrasse 28 🕐 Mon–Fri 10–6, Sat 10–3. Outlet: Tue 10–6 ☎ 713 69 60 🚇 U3 to Rochusgasse 🚌 Bus 4A to Rochusgasse; tram O to Sechskrügelgasse

PISCHINGER

pischinger.at

This family-run chocolatier offers a large range of products, one of which is a Viennese classic, the Pischinger Eck—a dark chocolate triangle with the original Pischinger nut-croquant filling. The business has been running since 1849.

🏠 H9 ✉ Wien Hauptbahnhof, Am Hauptbahnhof 1 🕐 Mon–Fri 9–9, Sat–Sun 10–6 🚇 U1 to Südtirolerplatz/Hauptbahnhof

---

TRACHTENMODE

The basis of traditional Austrian dress is peasant and hunting costume. Women wear *Dirndls*—dresses with full skirts and lace blouses with a bodice—perhaps topped by a velvet jacket. Men wear green cloth jackets with braided cuffs and lapels, sometimes with buttons made from antlers. The best *Trachtenmode* is normally reserved for special occasions such as festivals and dances.

Entertainment and Nightlife

ARNOLD SCHÖNBERG CENTER
schoenberg.at
Not only a concert hall, but also an archive library and exhibition hall dedicated to the founder of Viennese modernism.

🔲 G6 ✉ Schwarzenberg-platz 6 ☎ 712 18 88 🚋 Trams D, 2, 71 to Schwarzenbergplatz

CLUB SCHWARZENBERG
clubschwarzenberg.at
An enormous venue devoted to a diverse program of music from around the world. Evenings could involve anything from piano music, French chansons, folk to flamenco.

🔲 G6 ✉ Schwartzenberg-platz 10/1 ☎ 505 62 28 🕐 Thu–Sat 11pm–late 🚇 U1, U2, U4 to Karlsplatz 🚋 Tram 1 to Karlsplatz

KONZERTHAUS
konzerthaus.at
Opened in 1913, the building contains three concert halls: The Grosser Saal, for orchestral performances; and the Mozartsaal and Schubertsaal for chamber music, modern music and *Lieder* evenings. In summer there are twice-weekly selections of Mozart's music, played by musicians dressed in period costume.

🔲 G6 ✉ Lothringerstrasse 20 ☎ 242 002 🚇 U4 to Stadtpark

MUSIKVEREIN
musikverein.at
The Musikverein is famous for its superb acoustics and sumptuous gilded interior. The Wiener Philharmoniker's New Year's Day Concert is broadcast from here and the orchestra's Sunday concerts are a Viennese institution. During the week there are orchestral concerts in the Great Hall, and chamber music in the Brahmssaal.

🔲 F6 ✉ Bösendorferstrasse 12 ☎ 505 81 90 for tickets 🚇 U1, U2, U4 to Karlsplatz 🚋 Trams 1, D to Kärntner Ring

PALACES
The city's summer music festival, Wiener Musik-Sommer, offers graceful chamber music in some lovely baroque palaces, among them Palffy and Auersperg.

RADIOKULTURHAUS
radiokulturhaus.orf.at
All kinds of music, often in virtuoso performances, may be heard in the Austrian Broadcasting Company's (ORF) Broadcasting Hall or in the adjacent Kulturcafé.

🔲 F7 ✉ Argentinierstrasse 30a ☎ 501 70 377 🚇 U1 to Taubstummengasse 🚋 Tram D to Plösslgasse

URANIA
planetarium-wien.at
Max Fabiani's interesting late-Jugendstil building on the Danube Canal was restored a few years ago. A multicultural performance hall, it hosts cinema and puppet theater and has an observatory.

🔲 H4 ✉ Uraniastrasse 1 ☎ 89 174 150 000 🚇 U1, U4 to Schwedenplatz 🚋 Trams 1, 2 to Schwedenplatz

DRESSING UP AND DOWN
When going out on the tiles, the Viennese like to dress up as well as down. Looking like a tourist at the theater, opera, upscale restaurants and other more formal venues is frowned upon and don't even think about wearing shorts or jeans. However, smart-casual is fine for most places and for Beisl and Heuriger visits you can wear what you like. In the past the Viennese have preferred more classic clothes rather than the latest fashions, but this is changing.

Where to Eat

PRICES

Prices are approximate, based on a 3-course meal for one person.

€€€   over €40
€€   €20–€40
€   under €20

CASA ALBERTO (€)

casa-alberto.at

This restaurant, popular with journalists from the nearby ORF (Austrian Broadcasting Company) serves an odd combination of Italian and Mexican food. Thankfully the two come on totally separate menus! The Italian fare is of better quality—the pizzas are particularly good.

➕ F7 ✉ Argentinierstrasse 15 ☎ 505 71 76
🕐 Daily 11–10 Ⓤ U1 to Taubstummengasse
🚋 Tram D to Gusshausstrasse

CAFE AM HEUMARKT (€)

Escape the tourists at this time-capsule café at the southern corner of the Stadtpark, where excellent coffees and Viennese essentials come with a smile. This place is open early enough for breakfast and late enough for a glass of something special, so come for both.

➕ G5 ✉ Am Heumarkt 15 ☎ 712 65 81
🕐 Mon–Fri 9am–11pm 🚋 U-Bahn Stadtpark

KLEIN STEIERMARK (€€)

kleinsteiermark.wien

A relaxing informal hostelry that offers specialties from the province of Styria. Try the *Mistfuhre* (literally "a load of rubbish"), which consists of grilled and fried meat with vegetables. In summer the garden with its adjacent playground is ideal for a family outing.

➕ H9 ✉ Heeresmuseum-strasse 1 (in the Schweizer-garten) ☎ 799 58 83 🕐 Daily 11.30–11; 25, 26 Dec 11–3. Closed 24 Dec

and about 2 weeks after Christmas Ⓤ U1 to Südtirolerplatz/Hauptbahnhof 🚋 Trams O, 18 to Fasangasse

ROCHUSMARKT (€–€€)

Stacked high with fresh produce, this authentically Viennese market is the ideal stop-off for good-quality picnic supplies. You can also pop into one of the surrounding cafés for a light lunch. Some of the food stands are open until 11pm, making this a great spot for some Viennese after-dark street food.

➕ J6 ✉ Landstrasser Hauptstrasse 🕐 Mon–Fri 6am–7.30pm, Sat 6am–5pm 🚋 Tram 1 to Sechskrügelgasse

SALM BRÄU (€)

salmbraeu.com

Salm Bräu is a bustling wood-panelled beer cellar occupying a former monastery, its barrel ceiling decorated traditionally in wreaths of hops. It serves good-value hot and cold food and great beer, five types of which are brewed on the premises. They also distil their own brandy, which has won several awards.

➕ H7 ✉ Rennweg 8 ☎ 799 599 92
🕐 Daily 11am–midnight 🚋 Tram 71 to Unteres Belvedere

STEIRERECK (€€€)

steirereck.at

A distinguished restaurant in stunning premises in the Stadtpark, it's famous for the delicacy of its *Neue Wiener Küche* and its well-chosen wine list. Reserve in advance. The bar, Meierei, serves dairy-based light meals.

➕ H5 ✉ Am Heumarkt 2 ☎ 713 31 68
🕐 Restaurant: Mon–Fri 11.30–3, 6.30–11. Bar: Mon–Fri 8am–11pm, Sat–Sun 9–7 Ⓤ U3 to Stubentor or Landstrasse, U4 to Stadtpark (park exit)

Farther Afield

Vienna's suburbs were once home ground both for the nobility and for craftsmen, with residential areas, cemeteries and workshops. Just beyondthem lies the varied landscape of the Wienerwald and the water meadows of the Danube's floodplain.

Top 25

Danube Cruise	**94**
Hundertwasser-Haus and KunstHausWien	**95**
Kahlenberg	**96**
MuTh	**97**
Prater and Riesenrad	**98**
Schloss Schönbrunn	**99**
More to See	**100**
Excursions	**102**
Shopping	**105**
Entertainment and Nightlife	**105**
Where to Eat	**106**

KLOSTER-
NEUBURG

LANGENZERSDORF

Wiener

Wald

Weidlingbach

Kahlenberg

Donauinsel

Donau

Neue Donau

NUSSDORF

GRINZING

NEUSTIFT
AM WALDE

SIEVERING

DÖBLING

PÖTZLEINSDORF

BRIGITTENAU

Franz-Josefs-
Bahnhof

NEUWALDEGG

WÄHRING

Augarten

MuTh

DORNBACH

HERNALS

ALSERGRUND

OTTAKRING

**Kirche am
Steinhof**

JOSEFSTADT

WIEN

HÜTTELDORF

223

PENZING

RUDOLFSHEIM-
FÜNFHAUS

NEUBAU

MARIA-
HILF

Westbahnhof

WIEDE

HACKING

**Technisches
Museum**

MARGARETEN

HIETZING

**Schloss
Schönbrunn**

221

Hauptbahnhof

224

MEIDLING

12

*Lainzer
Tiergarten*

225

FAVORITEN

225

SPEISING

0   3 km

0   2 miles

230

Wienerberg

A23

A23

MAUER

ATZGERSDORF

**Wotruba
Kirche**

LIESING

INZERSDORF

A2

12

ERLAA

13a

RODAUN

17

GERASDORF
BEI WIEN

STREBERSDORF

GROSS-
JEDLERSDORF

NEUSÜSSENBRUNN

A22

FLORIDSDORF

3

LEOPOLDAU

KAGRAN

8

302

52

52

BREITENLEE

DONAUSTADT

HIRSCH-
STETTEN

10

Alte Donau

KAISER-
MÜHLEN

Gänsehäufel

3b

Donau

A22

STADLAU

3

A23

*Prater &
Riesenrad*

LEOPOLDSTADT

ASPERN

KunstHausWien

Hundertwasser-Haus

Wittgenstein Haus

LANDSTRASSE

A23

Wiener
Strassenbahnmuseum

Donauinsel

Neue Donau

Lobau

10

Donau

ALBERN

225

SIMMERING

A4

225

Bestattungsmuseum

ROTH-
NEUSIEDL

10

OBERLAA

11

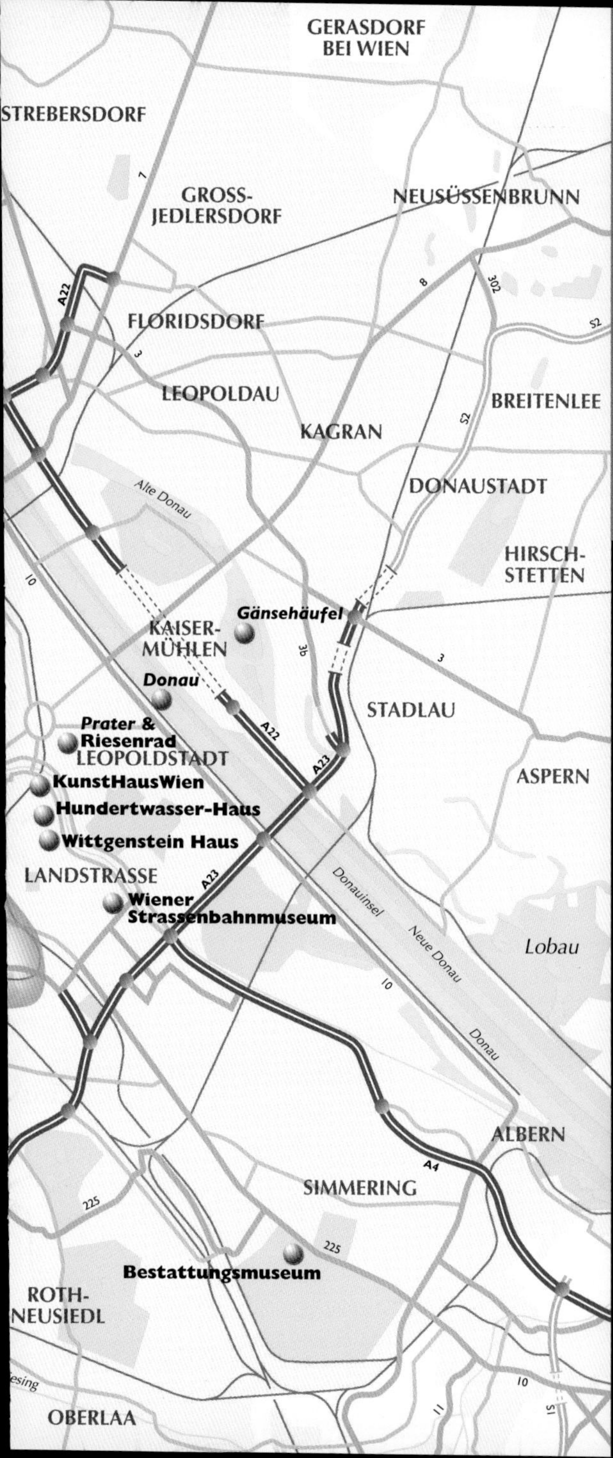

Danube Cruise

Cruising the Danube near Reichsbrücke (left); tour boat on the Donaukanal (right)

THE BASICS

➕ M1

Vienna Cruises

ddsg-blue-danube.at

☎ 58 880

🕓 Departures daily from Schwedenbrücke. Winter break (Nov–Mar)

💷 Expensive

Twin City Liner

twincityliner.com

☎ 58 880

🕓 Several departures daily from Schweden-brücke. Weekends only mid-Oct to Dec; winter break Jan to mid-Mar

♿ Good; advance reservation essential

💷 Expensive

❓ Advance reservations recommended. See website for departures and border formalities for Slovakia

NationalparkBoot

☎ 400 049 495 (booking required)

🕓 2 May–26 Oct daily at 9 near Salztorbrücke. Cruise is 4 hours with 1 hour walk

💷 Moderate

HIGHLIGHTS

● UNO-City (the towering UN headquarters)

● Kahlenberg and other hills

● The Secessionist Nussdorf Lock and Lock House

Leaving from the Schwedenplatz' striking ferry terminal, taking a couple of hours for a Danube cruise is a relaxing way to see the city from a different perspective, the city center and other locations lined up on the banks as you drift smoothly by.

River cruises There are also special cruises, mainly in the evenings, offering music and dancing. Also leaving from the northwestern end of Schwedenplatz (at Salztorbrücke) is the NationalparkBoot, which takes you to the Danube National Park and its water meadows. The park begins inside the city's boundaries and extends as far as the Slovak border.

Twin City Liner A cruise on the Twin City Liner is an experience worth having. In little more than an hour, this huge catamaran rushes you to Bratislava, capital of the Slovak Republic. It costs twice the price of the train journey but it's convenient as you start and arrive right in the heart of both cities.

Donauinsel The artificial island between the Old and the New Danube has become popular for biking, picnicking and (at its southern tip) for nudism. One weekend in June each year, the island hosts what is said to be Europe's biggest outdoor festival of pop music (free access). There are modestly priced restaurants around the "Copa Cagrana" between U1 stations Donauinsel and Kaisermühlen VIC.

TOP 25

Hundertwasser-Haus and KunstHausWien

Hundertwasser's career as an amateur architect began with his now-famous Hundertwasser-Haus in Vienna's Third District. It was built with the help of a professional architect, Josef Krawina, and opened in 1985.

The artist Born Friedrich Stowasser in 1928, the partly Jewish artist survived Nazi persecution in his native city of Vienna. In 1949, he took the name "Friedensreich Hundertwasser" and in 1953 painted the first of his colorful spirals. Over the years he became more and more involved in ecological initiatives as part of his artistic credo. He died on board the *Queen Elizabeth II* following a trip to New Zealand in 2000 and was buried there in his Garden of the Happy Dead—without a coffin, but with a tulip tree planted above his remains.

Hundertwasser-Haus The building reflects his opposition to pure functionalism and his view that "the straight line is godless." The house is not accessible (it's a block of flats). Instead, "Hundertwasser Village" across the street offers visitors the full Hundertwasser experience in all its whimsicality. There are souvenir shops, a bar and a restaurant with a pleasant garden terrace.

KunstHausWien The KunstHaus is in a former furniture factory close to the Hundertwasser-Haus. It was refurbished by the artist and now offers a survey of his life and work. Exhibitions pay homage to his unconventionality.

THE BASICS

Hundertwasser-Haus
hundertwasserhaus.info
+ J4
✉ Kegelgasse 34/ Löwengasse 41
👁 View from outside only
🚊 Tram 1 to Hetzgasse
♿ Good

KunstHausWien
kunsthauswien.com
+ J4
✉ Untere Weissgerberstrasse 13
☎ 712 04 91
🕐 Daily 10–6
🍴 Café-restaurant
🚊 Trams 1, O to Radetzkyplatz
♿ Good; ask at ticket office
🎟 Moderate

TIP

● You can cruise the Danube from Schwedenplatz in MS *Vindobona*, renovated by Hundertwasser in 1995.

FARTHER AFIELD TOP 25

Kahlenberg

Karl-Marx-Hof the tenement complex in Vienna

THE BASICS

See map ▷ 92
U4 to Heiligenstadt then bus 38A

Beethoven Houses
Testament Museum:
Probusgasse 6
Tue–Sun 10–1, 2–6
Restaurant Mayer:
Pfarrplatz 2
Mon–Fri from 4–12, Sat–Sun 12–12
Tram 37 to Geweygasse

Secessionist Villa Colony
Steinfeldgasse 2, 4, 6, 7; Wollergasse 10
Tram 37 to Hohe Warte

HIGHLIGHTS

● View from Kahlenberg
● Karl-Marx-Hof tenement block

TIP

● The Heurigen Express (heurigenexpress.at) is an open-top hop-on/hop-off shuttle bus connecting Nussdorf (Tram D) and Kahlenberg (Apr–Oct daily 12–6 every hour, moderate).

When you've had enough of Vienna's bustle, head to the hills north of the city to sample Austrian wine in a village tavern and admire some architecture.

Kahlenberg Imperial troops and their allies gathered here before liberating Vienna from the Turkish siege in 1683. The hill has become a very popular place from which to view the panorama of Vienna. In the small Sobieski Chapel a fresco recalls the Polish contribution to the liberation of Vienna.

Heiligenstadt Heiligenstadt is famous for the Heiligenstadt Testament, a letter written by an ailing Beethoven to his brothers. If this depresses you, restore your spirits with a glass of wine in the Beethoven House on Pfarrplatz.

Hohe Warte Secessionist Villa Colony Josef Hoffmann was a leading light of the Vienna Secession and co-founder of the Wiener Werkstätte. Four of his villas are located above Heiligenstadt's St. Michael's Church.

Karl-Marx-Hof Opposite the Heiligenstadt U-Bahn station is the most impressive dwelling-house of the 1920s "Red Vienna" period. Over 0.6 miles (1km) in length, it is the longest residential building in the world and once held 1,382 apartments. Many of these "workers' fortresses" played a significant role in the 1934 Civil War between authoritarian Conservative and Social Democratic forces.

The MuTh building is a combination of existing baroque structures and modern architecture

MuTh

The MuTh (Musik and Theater) opened at the end of 2012 as a concert hall for classical music and music theater. It's now also the permanent home of the Vienna Boys' Choir.

Vienna Boys' Choir Arguably the best-known choir of its kind in the world, the Wiener Sängerknaben was established more than 500 years ago as a church choir for Emperor Maximilian I. It has around 100 singers, from 10 to 14 years of age. Members come from Austria and around the world. The choir is divided into four touring groups, named after famous composers: Bruckner, Haydn, Mozart and Schubert.

Repertoire In the past, the choir performed mainly sacred and classical music, but in recent years the group has come under some pressure to diversify and modernize its repertoire. These days, expect anything from traditional Mozart and Haydn to pop and world music, such as a series of performances of Native American music. In addition to the MuTh, the choir regularly performs at the Vienna State Opera (▷ 35) and Burgkapelle (▷ 26). Check online for an updated performance schedule.

MuTh As well as hosting the Vienna Boys' Choir, the MuTh offers a wide-ranging program of classical music, modern dance, ballet and much more. Many performances are aimed at younger audiences.

THE BASICS

muth.at;
wienersaenger
knaben.at
🚹 G2
✉ Am Augartenspitz 1
(corner of Castellezgasse)
☎ 347 80 80
🕐 Box office: Mon–Fri
4–6
🚇 U2 to Taborstrasse
🚋 Tram 2 to Taborstrasse,
tram 31 to Obere
Augartenstrasse
♿ Some wheelchair
spaces
💰 Moderate

TIP

● Try to book your tickets as far in advance as possible as Vienna Boys' Choir performances are very popular.

Prater and Riesenrad

TOP 25

The giant ferris wheel and rides at the funfair on Prater

THE BASICS

prater.at;
wienerriesenrad.com

🔲 K2 (Prater M5)

✉ East of Praterstern

☎ 729 20 00

🕐 Funfair: 15 Mar–Oct daily. Ferris wheel: Daily from 9 or 10am until dusk.

🚇 U1, U2 to Praterstern

🚊 Trams O, 5 to Praterstern

♿ Good

🎫 Ferris wheel: Moderate; *Liliputbahn*: inexpensive. Combined tickets available

HIGHLIGHTS

● Ferris wheel
● *Liliputbahn*

TIP

● Take the *Liliputbahn* to Stadion, stroll down the Hauptallee and enjoy food at the Lusthaus (closed Wed).

The former imperial hunting grounds were opened to the public in 1766, and now include a chestnut avenue, a fairground and other leisure facilities. The world-famous amusement park has many diversions: The *Riesenrad* (Ferris wheel) is among the best known.

The big wheel The giant ferris wheel on the Prater, built in 1896 by Englishman Walter Basset, was where Harry Lime, played by Orson Welles, met his old friend in the film *The Third Man*. The wheel rotates at 75cm (29in) per second and offers great views across the city. Compartments can be hired for private celebrations and you can even get married in one.

Amusement park There has been ongoing debate between the entrepreneurs of the different attractions and the City of Vienna regarding the future of the "Wurstelprater" funfair. Some wish to retain its traditional character, others want to modernize it. In fact traditional and new elements can be found here. Attractions include the *Geisterbahn* (ghost train), the old-fashioned *Ringelspiel* (merry-go-round) and the narrow-gauge *Liliputbahn* (381mm/15in), which starts just behind the giant ferris wheel. There are new dodgems and various "test your strength" booths. Fans of old and new meet on the neutral ground of the *Schweizerhaus* (Swiss House) to sample its notoriously gigantic *Stelze* (knuckle of pork) served with Czech beer.

View of the palace from the formal gardens

TOP
25

Schloss Schönbrunn

Schönbrunn palace is one of Austria's finest, designed specifically to show off just how many rooms a great monarch could afford. The palace and park are now a UNESCO World Heritage Site containing a zoo and other attractions for children.

Pacassi's palace The original designs for an imperial residence in the hunting park with the beautiful spring (the *schöner Brunn*) were made by Johann Bernhard Fischer von Erlach in 1695. It was only partly built when Maria Theresa's court architect, Nikolaus Pacassi, revamped the design in the 1740s. His long, symmetrical palace is a vast corridor of gilded and crimson displays—Japanese, Italian, Persian and Indian works of art, ceiling frescoes celebrating the Habsburgs, and 18th-century furniture and porcelain. The palace looks out on a park with immaculate ornamental gardens complete with pools and fountains.

The park The 18th-century gardens were later partially restyled by Adrian van Steckhoven. On top of the hill is the Gloriette, a piece of pure architecture, originally with no interior (a café has since been installed). It is worth climbing up to it for the view over the city. The zoo has retained its 18th-century plan with a baroque pavilion in the middle, but now includes modern enclosures and buildings. Other additions are a spectacular 19th-century glasshouse and a labyrinth for kids in the restored maze.

THE BASICS

schoenbrunn.at
➕ See map ▷ 92
☎ 811 13 239
🕐 Palace: Apr–Jun, Sep, Oct daily 8.30–5; Jul, Aug 8.30–6; Nov–Mar 8.30–4.30. Carriage museum: Apr–Oct daily 9–6, Nov–Mar 10–4. Zoo: Apr–Sep daily 9–6.30; Nov–Jan 9–4.30; Feb 9–5; Mar, Oct 9–5.30. Park: Daily 6.30–dusk
🍽 Cafés and restaurants
🚇 U4 to Schönbrunn or Hietzing (for palm house and zoo)
🚌 Bus 10A; trams 10, 58 to Schönbrunn
♿ Good
💲 Palace, zoo: expensive; carriage museum: moderate; park: free
❓ Audio guides. Tours can be booked online

HIGHLIGHTS

● Carriage museum
● Oriental panels, Vieux-Lacque Room
● Mirrors and frescoed ceiling in the Great Gallery
● Park and Gloriette

TIP

● The Roman Ruin, an artistic fake symbolizing the victory of Rome over Carthage, is close to the *schöner Brunn* (the "beautiful spring").

FARTHER AFIELD TOP 25

More to See

AUGARTEN
augarten.at
Joseph II opened these gardens to the public in 1775. The porcelain factory in the Augarten Palace can be visited. The Augarten is also often host to the Vienna Boys' Choir and an annexe of the Belvedere collection, Augarten Contemporary.
➕ G1 🕙 Park: 6am–dusk
Porcelain Museum ✉ Obere Augartenstrasse 1A ☎ 211 24 200 🕙 Mon–Sat 10–6 🚇 U2 to Taborstrasse 🚊 Tram 2 to Taborstrasse/Obere Augartenstrasse 🎫 Inexpensive

BESTATTUNGSMUSEUM
bestattungsmuseum.at
This museum is near the main entrance to the city's Central Cemetery (Zentralfriedhof). Exhibits focus on Viennese funeral and burial practices using photographs and objects, as well as interactive video presentations.
➕ See map ▷ 93 ✉ Wiener Zentralfriedhof Tor 2, Simmeringer Hauptstrasse 234 ☎ 760 67 🕙 Mon–Fri 9–4.30,

Relaxing in Augarten

Sat Mar–Oct 10–5.30 🚊 Trams 6, 71 to Zentralfriedhof (Haupttor) 🎫 Moderate

GÄNSEHÄUFEL
gaensehaeufel.at
This is the Lido of Vienna, an island in the Alte Donau (Old Danube), the now-dead arm of the river. Facilities include an open-air pool with artificial waves and a water-chute, tennis, minigolf and even a place where rock climbers can try their skills. It can be extremely crowded on hot summer days.
➕ See map ▷ 93 ✉ Moissigasse 21 ☎ 269 90 16 🕙 May–Sep Mon–Fri 9–8, Sat–Sun 8–8 🚇 U1 to Kaisermühlen VIC (Vienna International Centre), then bus 92A to Schüttauplatz or occasional shuttle services ♿ Good 🎫 Moderate

KIRCHE AM STEINHOF
The weird and wonderful Steinhof Church was built by Otto Wagner for patients with mental illnesses in 1907. The interior is clinically white with special fittings, full of wonders from Secession artists—most notably Kolo Moser's glass-mosaic windows.
➕ See map ▷ 92 ✉ Sozialmedizinisches Zentrum, Baumgartner Höhe 1 ☎ 910 60 11 007 🕙 Sat 4–5, Sun 12–4 (open access). Guided tour in German Sat 3pm, Sun 4pm or by prior arrangement 🚌 Buses 47A, 48A to Psychiatrisches Zentrum ♿ None 🎫 Tours inexpensive for groups of 10 people or more; expensive for smaller groups and tours in English

TECHNISCHES MUSEUM
technischesmuseum.at
Here you can explore the inventions and technical development of Austria past and present.

The museum displays its items in user-friendly and spacious settings.
➕ See map ▷ 92 ✉ Mariahilferstrasse 212 ☎ 89998-0 🕓 Mon–Fri 9–6, Sat–Sun, hols 10–6 🍴 Café 🚊 Trams 52, 58 from U3 Westbahnhof to Penzinger Strasse ♿ Good 💶 Moderate

WIENER STRASSENBAHNMUSEUM
tram.at
A family-friendly option for those keen on trains; noteworthy in the Tramway Museum are the horse- and steam-driven trams of the 19th century and a New York streetcar. Vintage tram carriages can be hired for special occasions.
➕ L7 ✉ Ludwig-Kössler-Platz ☎ 790 941 800 🕓 May–early Oct Sat–Sun, hols 10–5 🚇 U3 to Schlachthausgasse 🚌 Bus 77A to Ludwig-Kössler-Platz; tram 18 to Schlachthausgasse 💶 Moderate

WITTGENSTEIN HAUS
haus-wittgenstein.at
Ludwig Wittgenstein, one of the most famous philosophers of the 20th century, designed this austere house for his sister in the 1920s. The house reflects its creator's intellect; built in the Bauhaus style, it is curious rather than architecturally appealing. It is now owned by the government of Bulgaria and is used as the Bulgarian Cultural Institute.
➕ J5 ✉ Parkgasse 18 ☎ 713 31 64 🕓 Mon–Thu 10–5 🚇 U3 to Rochusgasse 💶 Free

WOTRUBA KIRCHE
georgenberg.at
This extraordinary modern church, designed by the sculptor Fritz Wotruba and constructed in 1976, seems to have been assembled with randomly jumbled concrete blocks and lit by arbitrarily placed narrow glass panels.
➕ See map ▷ 92 ✉ Georgsgasse/ Rysergasse (Mauer, 23rd District) ☎ 888 61 47. Guided tours 650 332 4833 🕓 Sat and before church hols 2–8, Sun 9–5 🚊 Tram 60 to Maurer Hauptplatz, then bus 60A to Kaserngasse

Wotruba Kirche

Excursions

BADEN

THE BASICS

baden.at
Distance: 16 miles (25km)
Journey Time: 1 hour
☎ Tourist Office: 02252/ 22 600-600
🚃 Badner Bahn (blue-white tram) from Oper. Supplementary fare from Vienna's city border
❓ Operetta performances in the Stadttheater end Jun to mid-Sep

A geological fault where the eastern edge of the Alps meets the Vienna Basin is responsible for the mineral springs at Baden, first exploited by the Romans. The now-sleepy town became a fashionable spa during the Biedermeier period (1815–48).

In the early 19th century, the Habsburg court under Emperor Franz I used Baden as its imperial summer residence. Mozart wrote his sublime *Ave Verum* chorus for the choir of the parish church. The town is full of Joseph Kornhäusel's neoclassical architecture. Both a tram (*Lokalbahn*) and bus service run from Oper to Baden (16 miles/ 25km).

BRATISLAVA

THE BASICS

bratislava.sk
Distance: 43 miles (70km)
Journey Time: 1 hour
🚆 From Wien Hauptbahnhof to Bratislava Hlavná stanica (Main Station) or Petrzalka twice every hour
🚢 Twin City Liner (▷ 94)

For 1,000 years a part of Hungary and for more than two centuries its capital, Bratislava became the capital of the newly independent Slovak Republic in 1993.

While the old city core has preserved its medieval and baroque charm, the outskirts of Bratislava have boomed since the fall of the Iron Curtain in 1989. A highlight is St. Martin's Cathedral, where 11 kings of Hungary were crowned. The views over the city from either the castle terraces or the tower of the Novy most (New Bridge) are spectacular.

HEILIGENKREUZ

THE BASICS

stift-heiligenkreuz.org
Distance: 22 miles (35km)
Journey Time: 1 hour
☎ 022 58 870 30
🚆 From Wien Hauptbahnhof (U1) or Wien Meidling (U6) to Mödling, then bus 365
🕐 Mon–Sat at 10, 11, 2, 3, 4. Sun, hols no tour at 10
💶 Moderate

This abbey, whose name "Holy Cross" is derived from the fragment of the True Cross preserved in a tabernacle on the main altar, was founded in 1133 by the Cistercians.

The beautiful medieval church has a lovely Romanesque nave and Gothic cloister. The cloister dates from the mid-13th century and, as such, marks the transition from Romanesque to early Gothic architecture. Later baroque features include the Trinity Column and St. Joseph Fountain in the courtyard, by Giovanni Giuliani (1664–1744). Visits are by guided tour only, which must be arranged in advance. It's also possible to stay the night as a guest.

KLOSTERNEUBURG

Legend has it that this monastery was founded on the spot where Margrave Leopold III discovered the veil of his wife Agnes after the wind had blown it away when they were out hunting.

The small winegrowers' town upstream from the capital was the residence of the Babenbergs in the 12th century, before they moved to Vienna. In the 18th century, Charles VI planned to turn it into an Austrian Escorial. The Verdun altar with its gilded copper plates from 1181 and the "Archduke's hat," the modest crown of the Duchy of Austria, are the most interesting exhibits. Another attraction in the town is the private Essl Collection of contemporary art (An der Donau-Au 1, tel 02243-370 50-150, Tue–Sun 10–6, Wed 10–9, moderate, Wed 5–9pm free).

THE BASICS

stift-klosterneuburg.at
Distance: 6 miles (10km)
Journey Time: 20 min by train or bus
☎ 022 43 41 10
🚌 Bus 238, 239 from Heiligenstadt to Klosterneuburg-Kierling
🚆 From Spittelau (U4, U6) to Klosterneuburg-Kierling
Monastery
🕐 May–Nov daily 9–6, Dec–Apr 10–4. Dec 24, 31 12–4; Jan 1 1–4
♿ Moderate

LAXENBURG

The former imperial summer resort at Laxenburg has three palaces to visit and an extensive English park.

You come first to the baroque Blue Court (which is not blue at all). Inside the park, to the right, is the Old Palace, and to your left is the 19th-century neo-Gothic folly known as the Franzensburg. The latter boasts a fake medieval dungeon, complete with a knight in chains and realistic groans in the background. It is on an island reached by a cable ferry, or via a bridge from the rear of the park. You can also take a rowboat and discover the hidden beauties of the lake, including a vast romantic grotto.

The Old Palace now houses the Austrian Film Archive, while the Blue Court is the seat of the IIASA, the International Institute for Applied Systems Analysis. In the lavish surroundings of a former imperial pleasure ground, experts ponder the problems of today's environmental, economic and social changes. In early June the grounds and palaces are home to the annual Laxenburg Spring Festival, which features opera, modern music and music theater.

THE BASICS

laxenburg.at
schloss-laxenburg.at
Distance: 16 miles (25km)
Journey Time: 30 min
🚌 Bus 566 from U1 Wien Hauptbahnhof, hourly
☎ 02236/71101-0
🕐 Park: Daily dawn–dusk. Franzensburg: Easter–Oct daily 11, 2, 3
♿ Park, ferry, Franzensburg tour: Inexpensive. Panorama train: Moderate

MELK AND THE WACHAU VALLEY

The huge baroque monastery at Melk
commands the entrance to the Wachau Valley
on the Danube. You can take a cruise either
from Melk downstream to Krems in the Wachau
or from Krems upstream to Melk. Stroll through
the narrow streets of Krems or see an art
exhibition in the Kunsthalle. The river valley,
which is a UNESCO World Heritage Site, is
adorned with vineyards, picturesque villages
and medieval castle ruins. The most famous of
these is hill-top Dürnstein, where the English
King Richard the Lionheart was held prisoner
from 1192 to 1193. The views from the ruined
ramparts are spectacular.

SEEGROTTE HINTERBRÜHL

Situated in a former gypsum mine, this is
Europe's biggest underground lake. Water
accumulated in it after an accident during a
blasting operation in 1912, and has to be
pumped out daily (there are seven sources but
no outflow). During World War II, the grotto was
taken over by the German military and used to
house an underground aircraft factory because
of the protection the cave afforded against
frequent Allied bombing raids. Nowadays,
the grotto is a popular attraction, with visitors
cruising the waters in small boats.

SEMMERING

Completed in 1854, the Semmering railway,
which runs southwest from Vienna to the
Italian border, was the first mountain railway
on the continent. It is still admired for its
sophisticated engineering in a mountainous
landscape. In the early 20th century Semmering
was a summer retreat for the well-to-do from
Vienna and Budapest, and Semmering station
still exudes a resort atmosphere. In 1998,
Semmering Railway was added to the
UNESCO World Heritage list. Every few years,
the World Cup downhill ski races take place
on the Hirschenkogel at the top of the
Semmering pass.

Shopping

HUNDERTWASSER VILLAGE

hundertwasser-village.com

Possibly the best place in Vienna to buy colorful prints and other items relating to the artist and architect Hundertwasser. There are number of small gift shops within the interesting buildling as well as a small gallery.

➕ J4 ✉ Kegelgasse 37–39 ☎ 710 41 16 ⏰ Daily 9–6 🚊 Tram 1 to Hetzgasse

MANNER FACTORY OUTLET

Locally produced Neopolitan wafers are sold in attractive gift packs, and Ildefonso chocolates are offered at a small shop attached to the factory.

➕ Off map at A3 ✉ Wilhelminestrasse 6 ☎ 488 22-3770 ⏰ Mon–Fri 9–5 🚊 Tram 44 to Wilhelminenstrasse

WIENER PORZELLANFABRIK

augarten.at

Here you can buy beautiful Augarten porcelain direct from the factory. For those looking for a bargain, seconds sell at a 20 percent discount.

➕ G1 ✉ Wiener Porzellanmanufaktur, Obere Augartenstrasse 1A ☎ 211 24 200 ⏰ Mon–Fri 10–6 🚊 Tram 2 to Obere Augartenstrasse

COSTLY LEATHER

Fashion items such as leather goods are expensive in Vienna. The best selections and prices are found at chain stores like Humanic, in the shopping mall on the southern outskirts of the city (✉ Shopping City Süd, Vösendorf 🚌 Ikea bus from the Oper).

Entertainment and Nightlife

FRITZ EPPEL

eppel-boote.at

A great way to relax from the city hustle and bustle is to rent a boat from Fritz Eppel and take to the Alte Donau under your own steam.

➕ Off map at L1 ✉ Wagramer Strasse 48A ☎ 263 3530 🚇 U1 to Alte Donau

SCHÖNBRUNNER SCHLOSSTHEATER

kammeroper-schoenbrunn.at

Music students perform lighter opera and operettas here in July and August. This was one of the first palace theaters in Europe dating back to 1747.

➕ Off map at A9 ✉ Schloss Schönbrunn ☎ 664 1111 600 🚇 U4 to Schönbrunn

U4

u-4.at

An enduring dance club with live music and theme nights. Next door is a bar.

➕ Off map at A9 ✉ Schönbrunner Strasse 222–228 ☎ 664 948 15 12 ⏰ Mon–Tue, Thu–Sat 10pm–5am 🚇 U4 to Meidlinger Hauptstrasse

WIENER STADTHALLE

stadthalle.com

This sports complex with an ice rink and Olympic-size pool stages concerts, shows and exhibitions.

➕ A5/6 ✉ Roland-Rainer-Platz 1 ☎ 79 999 79 ⏰ Mon–Fri 1.30–5, Sat–Sun, hols 8–12, 1–5 🚇 U6 to Burggasse 🚊 Tram 18 to Burggasse/Stadthalle

Where to Eat

DOMMAYER (€€)

oberlaa-wien.at

This is Vienna's oldest music café. Once a month, the female ensemble Wiener Walzmädchen gives a performance. Johann Strauss once played here.

🔲 Off map at A9 ✉ Auhofstrasse 2 (Hietzing) ☎ 877 54 65-0 ⏲ Daily 7.30am–8.30pm 🚋 Tram 58 to Dommayergasse

DONAUTURM (€€€)

donauturm.at

Dine in the revolving restaurant at the top of the Danube Tower. The kitchen specializes in traditional Austrian dishes. Reservations are required.

🔲 Off map at L1 ✉ Donauturmstrasse 4 ☎ 263 35 72 ⏲ Daily 11.30–4, 6–2; observation deck: 10am–midnight 🚌 Bus 20B from U1 Kaisermühlen VIC to Donauturm (watch for direction)

FUHRGASSL-HUBER (€€)

fuhrgassl-huber.at

One of the most congenial taverns in Neustift's long main street offers a warm welcome. The same family also runs an excellent pension close by.

🔲 Off map at D1 ✉ Neustift am Walde 68 ☎ 440 14 05 ⏲ Mon–Sat 2pm–midnight, Sun, hols 12–12 🚇 U4, U6 to Spittelau then bus 35A to Neustift am Walde

MAYER AM PFARRPLATZ (€€)

pfarrplatz.at

This is the most famous Heuriger in Heiligenstadt, where Beethoven is said to have worked on his Ninth Symphony. There's music from 7pm and a huge tasty buffet.

🔲 Off map at D1 ✉ Heiligenstädter Pfarrplatz 2 ☎ 370 12 87 ⏲ Mon–Sat 4–midnight, Sun 12–12. Closed Christmas to mid-Jan 🚇 U4 to Heiligenstadt then bus 38A to Fernsprechamt/Pfarrplatz

PLACHUTTA (€€€)

plachutta.at

If you want to sample the famous Wiener Tafelspitz (boiled beef) at its most luxurious, as well as other beef specialties, this is the place. The restaurant is in the suburb of Hietzing, close to Schönbrunn, with another outlet in the Innere Stadt at Wollzeile 38.

🔲 Off map at A9 ✉ Auhofstrasse 1 ☎ 877 70 87 ⏲ Daily 11.30–3, 6–11.30. Closed mid-Jul to mid-Aug 🚇 U4 to Hietzing 🚋 Tram 58 to Dommayergasse

WILD (€€)

gasthaus-wild.at

A characterful restaurant with excellent traditional Austrian food and friendly service. Its large terrace is in the shadow of a rail bridge, but you don't notice it.

🔲 J4 ✉ Radetzkyplatz 1 ☎ 920 94 77 ⏲ Mon–Sat 10am–midnight, Sun 11.30am–10pm 🚋 Tram 1 to Radetzkyplatz

HEURIGEN

A Heuriger is a tavern in its own vineyard, traditionally selling only the current year's Heuer (wine). When open, a Heuriger is ausg'steckt, indicated by a bunch of fir twigs hung outside the door. The basic wine is Gemischter Satz, a white blend of local grapes. Roast meats, cheeses and salads are served in most Heurigen. The warm atmosphere is quintessentially Viennese, with Schrammelmusik playing.

Where to Stay

In Vienna there is an extremely broad choice of hotels, and many succeed in combining old-fashioned charm with modern comfort.

Introduction **108**
Budget Hotels **109**
Mid-Range Hotels **110**
Luxury Hotels **112**

Introduction

Vienna has it all when it comes to getting your head down. From luxury hotels in baroque palaces to time-warped family-run guesthouses, there's a place to stay for every budget.

Tradition

At the crossroads of Central Europe, Vienna has a long tradition of welcoming guests, from medieval crusaders and merchants to the high-ranking diplomats, officials of international bodies and tourists of today. The names of some hotels—such as Ambassador, König von Ungarn (King of Hungary), Das Triest or Imperial—reflect the city's ancient geographical and historical significance. To stay in one of these is to be transported back in time. These traditional hotels have nevertheless been tastefully modernized, so they fully meet the demands of today's traveler.

Millionaires and Expense Accounts

Vienna has become a top venue for international conferences and is one of the three bases of the UN. The OPEC headquarters are located here and the city attracts well-to-do and influential visitors from Arab nations. The new millionaires from the post-Communist countries of Eastern Europe, plus many of their compatriots, have also become regular visitors. To cater to this new clientele, recent hotel development has been in the mid-range and luxury categories.

HOTEL LOCATIONS

Most of the famous hotels are inside or on the Ringstrasse. This includes traditional 19th-century luxury hotels like Sacher, Imperial or Bristol, but also chain offerings from the likes of Marriot and Le Meridien. Hotels outside the Ringstrasse are less formal and often located on attractive smaller streets or courtyards. Hotels on the outskirts of the city may offer a more park-like environment or gardens, as well as lower prices. Hostels are mostly in the Inner Districts between the Ringstrasse and Gürtel (Ring Road).

From top: Viennese hotels: Kaiserin Elisabeth; views of Hotel Imperial; Hotel Sacher

Budget Hotels

DO STEP INN

dostepinn.at

This pleasant hotel offers a good location next to the Westbahnhof (West train station), as well as decent shopping and eating on Mariahilfer Strasse. It has a range of modest but clean singles, doubles and suites.

🏠 A6 ⊠ Felberstrasse 20 ☎ 982 33 14 🚇 U3, U6 to Westbahnhof

KUGEL

hotelkugel.at

Over a century old, Kugel is extremely good value and near the lively Spittelberg area, which is full of restaurants. While not a luxurious option, the rooms are modern yet charming and exceed what you'd expect for this price.

🏠 C5/6 ⊠ Siebensterngasse 43/Neubaugasse 46 ☎ 523 33 55 ⊕ Closed early Jan–early Feb 🚇 U3 to Neubaugasse 🚌 Bus 13A; tram 49 to Neubaugasse/Westbahnhofstrasse

LEHRERHAUS

hotel-lehrerhaus.at

Run by the Association for Teachers' Accommodation, this pension in the suburb of the Josefstadt sits just behind the Parliament and Rathaus. It has 40 rooms (33 en suite). Vienna's English Theatre is based in the same building.

🏠 D4 ⊠ Lange Gasse 20–22 Josefsgasse ☎ 403 23 58 🚇 U2 to Rathaus 🚌 Tram 2 to Rathaus

MARIAHILF HOTEL-PENSION

mariahilf-hotel.at

As inexpensive as you'll find in this location near the MuseumsQuartier, this pension has clean, airy, if somewhat dated rooms, sleeping between two and six people. There's a breakfast room, but no restaurant but this is no-fuss, honest option for those on a budget.

🏠 D6 ⊠ Mariahilferstrasse 49 ☎ 586 17 81 🚇 U3 to Neubaugasse

PENSION WILD

pension-wild.com

Traditionally one of the city's cheaper guesthouses, Pension Wild nevertheless offers an excellent location near the center in Josefstadt, with good public transportation links and comfortable rooms in a historic town house. The cheapest rooms come without en suite baths, though sinks with hot and cold water are available in every room.

🏠 D4 ⊠ Lange Gasse 10 ☎ 406 51 74 🚇 U3 to Volkstheater

TIME OUT CITY HOTEL

timeout.co.at

This modest bed-and-breakfast, within easy walking distance of the MuseumsQuartier, combines the best of a family-run atmosphere with a location in a historic Jugendstil (Secession) building. The public areas have been given a bright, modern makeover, though the decor in the bedrooms is more subdued.

🏠 D5 ⊠ Windmuehlgasse 6 ☎ 587 71 55 🚇 U3 to Neubaugasse

WHERE TO STAY BUDGET HOTELS

Mid-Range Hotels

25HOURS HOTEL VIENNA

25hours-hotel.com

The theme at this hotel is the theater and circus, and the rooms have been given a colorful retro makeover. The restaurant serves imaginative Mediterranean cuisine in an eye-catching, postmodern space.

🚇 D5 ✉ Lerchenfelder Strasse 1–3 ☎ 521 510 🚇 U2 to Volkstheater

ALMA BOUTIQUE HOTEL

hotel-alma.com

This mid-sized family-run design hotel meets the needs of tourist and business traveler alike. Rooms are modern without being overly brash, the hotel offers a buffet breakfast and the roof terrace is an added bonus.

🚇 G4 ✉ Hafnersteig 7 ☎ 533 29 610 🚇 U1, U4 to Schwedenplatz

ALTSTADT VIENNA

altstadt.at

The beautifully furnished upper floors of this late 19th-century house are an informal, friendly, breakfast-only hotel.

🚇 C5 ✉ Kirchengasse 41 ☎ 522 66 66 🚇 U2, U3 to Volkstheater 🚌 Bus 48A to Kellermanngasse

ALTWIENERHOF

altwienerhof.at

Bargain rates, in view of the fine restaurant. The rooms have an Belle Époque look and there is a lovely courtyard.

🚇 A8 ✉ Herklotzgasse 6 ☎ 892 60 00 🚇 U6 to Gumpendorfer Strasse 🚌 Bus 57A; trams 6, 18 to Gumpendorfer Strasse

BEST WESTERN PREMIER SCHLOSS-HOTEL RÖMISCHER KAISER

bestwestern.com

Housed in a modest baroque palace in the old city, this is a delightful place to stay, all crimson fabrics and sparkling chandeliers—it has an intimate feel.

🚇 F5 ✉ Annagasse 16 ☎ 512 77 510 🚇 U1, U3 to Stephansplatz

DAS CAPRI

dascapri.at

This medium-sized hotel in Leopoldstadt (across the Danube canal from the center) has big modern rooms, some with balconies, gleaming baths, a great breakfast buffet and a U-Bahn station just outside the front door to take you to the center in around five minutes.

🚇 H3 ✉ Praterstrasse 44–46 ☎ 214 84 04 🚇 U1 to Nestroyplatz

FLEMINGS HOTEL WIEN-WESTBAHNHOF

flemings-hotels.com

A four-star hotel with elegant rooms furnished in a contemporary style, that make a central feature of its glass-and-granite shower cubicles.

🚇 B6 ✉ Neubaugürtel 26–28 ☎ 227 370 🚇 U3 to Westbahnhof, U6 to Burggasse 🚋 Trams 5 to Burggasse, 18 to Westbahnhof

DAY AND NIGHT

The Viennese tend to get up early, but this works to the tourist's advantage, as public transportation will be much more comfortable when you are heading for your first sight. By the same token, many Viennese go relatively early to bed and lots of restaurants serve supper quite early. For night owls there are plenty of bars and a good network of night-long transport.

HOLLMANN BELETAGE HOTEL

hollmann-beletage.at

Designed to feel like a cutting-edge residential apartment, here guests are encouraged to relax as if they are at home. The six-course breakfast menu changes daily.

🔲 G4 ✉ Köllnerhofgasse 6 ☎ 96 11 960 🚇 U1, U4 to Schwedenplatz 🚊 Trams 1, 2 to Schwedenplatz

HOTEL RATHAUS WINE AND DESIGN

hotel-rathaus-wien.at

Each double room is dedicated to a different Austrian winemaker, and the staff will discuss the merits of different wines in the wine lounge.

🔲 D4 ✉ Lange Gasse 13 ☎ 400 11 22 🚇 U2 to Rathaus/Volkstheater, U3 to Volkstheater

HOTEL WANDL

hotel-wandl.com

A family-run hotel, next to Peterskirche in a partly 12th-century building. The rooms have a calm, comfortable and modern finish.

🔲 F4 ✉ Petersplatz 9 ☎ 534 550 🚇 U1, U3 to Stephansplatz

KÖNIG VON UNGARN

kvu.at

An 18th-century building next to the Figarohaus where the rooms ring an airy, glassed-in courtyard. It has a prestigious restaurant.

🔲 G4 ✉ Schulerstrasse 10 ☎ 515 840 🚇 U1, U3 to Stephansplatz

LANDHAUS FUHRGASSL-HUBER

landhaus-fuhrgassl-huber.at

This hotel is located in a wine village by the Vienna Woods. Elements within the rooms may be a little tired in places but its peasant-style furniture and summer courtyard make it special.

🔲 Off map at D1 ✉ Rathstrasse 24, Neustift am Walde ☎ 440 30 33 🚌 Bus 35A to Neustift am Walde

PENSION NOSSEK

pension-nossek.at

This hotel is located in the heart of the city; the pedestrianized area ensures quiet. The rooms range from spacious to compact and are basic but with antique furniture offering character.

🔲 F4 ✉ Graben 17 ☎ 533 704 111 🚇 U1, U3 to Stephansplatz

STEIGENBERGER HOTEL HERRENHOF

herrenhof-wien.steigenberger.at

This sleek, contemporary hotel is close to the Hofburg. Its restaurant serves good modern Viennese cuisine, and there's an atmospheric piano bar and café. It's at the top end of this mid-range bracket.

🔲 E4 ✉ Herrengasse 10 ☎ 534 040 🚇 U3 to Herrengasse

ZIPSER

zipser.at

The Zipser is a premium address for cultural tourists who also want to enjoy the special flair of Vienna's smartest suburb, Josefstadt. The area has a pleasant villagey atmosphere.

🔲 C3 ✉ Lange Gasse 49 ☎ 404 540 🚇 U2 to Rathaus

SUBURBS

While luxury hotels are clearly concentrated in the Inner City or Ringstrassen area, many mid-range ones are in the suburbs. Access to the city center is not a problem, as most of them are near U-Bahn or tram stations.

WHERE TO STAY MID-RANGE HOTELS

Luxury Hotels

PRICES
Expect to pay over €250 per night for a double room at a luxury hotel.

BRISTOL

bristolvienna.com

The Bristol offers old-fashioned elegance on the Ringstrasse. A recent refurbishment has given the rooms an overdue update. Some rooms have evocative views over the Opera.

🔢 F5 ✉ Kärntner Ring 1 ☎ 515 160
🚇 U1, U2, U4 to Karlsplatz/Oper

DO & CO HOTEL VIENNA

doco.com

There's a Turkish influence in the sumptuous styling of the rooms, and some interesting extras—including a TV in the bathroom, and both three- and two-pin plug sockets. The Do & Co restaurant (▷ 44) is superb.

🔢 F4 ✉ Stephansplatz 12 ☎ 24 188
🚇 U1, U3 to Stephansplatz

GRAND HOTEL WIEN

grandhotelwien.com

This Imperial-style hotel is one of the city's classics. Its celebrity guests range from Johann Strauss to Paul McCartney. Its top-class restaurants include Le Ciel and Unkai.

🔢 F5 ✉ Kärntner Ring 9 ☎ 515 800
🚇 U1, U2, U4 to Karlsplatz/Oper 🚋 Trams 1, 2, D to Opernring

HOTEL IMPERIAL

imperialvienna.com

This former palace is also the official State Hotel where dignitaries stay so you can expect regal styling and quality.

🔢 F6 ✉ Kärntner Ring 16 ☎ 501 100
🚇 U1, U2, U4 to Karlsplatz 🚋 Trams 2, D to Schwarzenbergplatz

HOTEL SACHER

sacher.com

This is Vienna's most celebrated hotel and the rooms are opulent and classically furnished. Sacher was founded in 1876 by the son of the cook to Prince Metternich and carried on by his widow, Anna, who ruled with an iron rod. Just after World War I, she single-handedly held off rioting workers, but she also had a strong social conscience and helped feed the poor.

🔢 F5 ✉ Philharmoniker-strasse 4 ☎ 514 565 55 🚇 U1, U2, U4 to Karlsplatz/Oper

PALAIS HANSEN KEMPINSKI VIENNA

kempinski.com/wien

This hotel occupies an imposing 19th-century palace. Amenities include two restaurants, a cigar lounge and a Turkish-style spa. Rooms are high-end and contemporary in look.

🔢 F3 ✉ Schottenring 24 ☎ 236 10 00
🚇 U2, U4 to Schottenring

THE RING

theringhotel.com

This classy, modern hotel, in a historic building, has a boutique feel. There is a spa and its restaurant, At Eight, is award winning.

🔢 F6 ✉ Kärntner Ring 8 ☎ 22 122 🚇 U1, U2, U4 to Karlsplatz/Oper 🚋 Trams 1, 2, D to Opernring

SOFITEL VIENNA STEPHANSDOM

sofitel.com

This relatively recent entry to the luxury category sits in the up-and-coming 2nd District, and has a striking design in glass and steel. There are panoramic views from the top-floor restaurant.

🔢 G3 ✉ Praterstrasse 1 ☎ 906 160 🚇 U3 to Schwedenplatz

Need to Know

This section supplies you with all the practical information needed to make your stay in Vienna as comfortable as possible, including tips for using public transport, when to go and money matters.

Planning Ahead **114**

Getting There **116**

Getting Around **118**

Essential Facts **120**

Language **122**

Timeline **124**

Planning Ahead

When to Go

Most of the important festivals and events are held in spring and summer. The main opera and concert seasons kick off in autumn. Some prime attractions (such as the Lipizzaners and the Vienna Boys' Choir) take a summer break and may be on tour some months.

AVERAGE DAILY MAXIMUM TEMPERATURES

JAN	FEB	MAR	APR	MAY	JUN	JUL	AUG	SEP	OCT	NOV	DEC
34°F	37°F	48°F	59°F	66°F	73°F	79°F	77°F	68°F	59°F	45°F	39°F
1°C	3°C	9°C	15°C	19°C	23°C	26°C	25°C	20°C	15°C	7°C	4°C

Spring (March to May) is rainy and sometimes fairly cool until mid-April.

Summer (June to August) seems to be getting hotter every year!

Autumn (September to October) is the most pleasant time to visit, when it is not too hot and mostly dry.

Winter (November to February) can be bitterly cold, often with heavy snow from late December.

If you suffer from migraines or circulation problems you may be affected by the *Föhn* wind blowing off the Alps.

WHAT'S ON

February *Opernball* (Opera Ball): The highlight of the social calendar.

March–April *OsterKlang*: Sacred music for Easter in St. Stephen's, the Musikverein and elsewhere.

February–June and September–December *Equestrian ballet*: Lipizzaner shows at the Hofburg.

April *Frühlingsfestival* (Mar/Apr to early May): Concerts in the Musikverein and Konzerthaus.

May *Maifest* (1 May): Celebrations mostly in the Prater.

Wiener Festwochen (May to mid-Jun): Arts festival in the MuseumsQuartier and other venues.

June *Open-air festival* (end Jun): Pop music on the Danube Island.

July *Jazz Fest Wien* (Jun–Jul): At the Opera House and various jazz clubs.

Operimsommer (Jul–Aug): Classical concerts and operas at the Theater an der Wien.

Music on Film (Jul–Sep): Films (mostly opera) on a screen before the Rathaus.

Summer Operetta (Jul–Aug): Schönbrunner Schlosstheater.

October *Viennale*: Film Festival.

Vienna Design Week: International design festival at various locations.

November *Wien Modern* (end Oct–Nov): One of Europe's biggest festivals of contemporary music.

November–December *Christkindlmarkt* (mid-Nov to 24 Dec): A Christmas fair in front of the Rathaus.

New Year's Eve *Silvesterpfad:* Shows and concerts.

Die Fledermaus: At the State Opera.

Vienna Online

vienna.info
Official site of the Vienna Tourist Board with information on sightseeing, eating out, culture and more. Useful for locating theater booking offices and (in some cases) booking online. The 72-hour itinerary is a good tour for first-time visitors and those with limited time.

austria.info
An easy-to-navigate site with information on all types of holiday in Austria, including car, motorcycle and hiking itineraries. Other features include a listing of events, weather forecasts, water temperatures in the lakes, plus webcam pictures of towns, landscapes and buildings.

wien.gv.at
This site offers diverse general information on the city, from politics and culture to urban development and the environment. Detailed map showing building numbers, one-way streets and City Bike stations (▷ 119).

aboutvienna.org
Alongside general information on the city, this English-language site offers focused sections on Viennese culture, cuisine, etiquette and the German language, as well as tips for those living and working in the city.

falter.at
Website for the weekly paper *Der Falter*, the city's best online resource for finding out what's happening around town. Dedicated sections on new movies, festivals, parties and events. In German only, but easy to navigate.

viennaconcerts.com
This website provides details of upcoming concert programs, and allows you to reserve tickets at the Staatsoper (State Opera) and other music venues in the city. There are packages available, and also a link to accommodations options.

TRAVEL SITES

fodors.com
A complete travel-planning site. Research prices and weather; book air tickets, cars and rooms; pose questions to fellow visitors; and find links to other sites.

oeamtc.at
Invaluable for motorists, this site (only in German) informs about the current state of traffic on Austrian roads, roadworks, weather conditions and much more. The visuals will help non-German speakers.

wienerlinien.at
The official website of the Wiener Linien, Vienna's public transportation authority. Handy information in English on tickets and fares, as well as a convenient online timetable to help plan journeys around town.

tourmycountry.com
Another website in English—although written by an Austrian—that has details on traveling and sightseeing in Austria, and aims to take a personal and opinionated approach.

Getting There

ENTRY REQUIREMENTS

Visitors from the UK, EU countries, the US and Canada need a passport (valid for at least six months) but do not need a visa. For the latest passport and visa information, check the relevant embassy website (Britain: bmeia.gv.at; US: austria.org).

Austria is part of the Schengen Zone. This means that there are no border restrictions for travel between countries that are part of the agreement (including adjacent countries Italy, Germany, Hungary, Czech Republic and Slovakia).

VACCINATIONS

Some wooded areas of Austria are home to *Zecken*, a kind of tick whose bite can transmit encephalitis, which in a few cases proves fatal. Enquire at the Austrian consulate about inoculation.

CUSTOMS REGULATIONS

Duty-free limits for non-European Union visitors are: 200 cigarettes or 250g of tobacco or 50 cigars; 4 liters of wine and 1 liter of spirits.

AIRPORT

Vienna International Airport (Flughafen Wien) is 19km (12 miles) east of the city at Schwechat. The airport has extensive shopping facilities, restaurants, bars, newsstands and car-rental desks.

ARRIVING BY AIR

The most convenient option for transportation to the city from Vienna International Airport (tel 700 70, viennaairport.com) is the Vienna Airport Lines bus (tel 70 07 32 300) to and from Vienna International Centre, Schwedenplatz and Westbahnhof (20–30 minutes, €8). The CAT express train (cityairporttrain. com) to Wien Mitte costs €12 and runs from 5.36am to 11.35pm; journey time 16 minutes. The S-Bahn (Schnellzug) rapid transit service is slower (24 minutes) but cheaper (€4.20) and runs from the Flughafen via Wien Mitte to Floridsdorf. Timetables of the above services are shown on the airport website. Taxis from the airport cost between €35 and €45.

ARRIVING BY TRAIN

Trains are operated by the Austrian Federal Railways (Österreichische Bundesbahn/ÖBB). The ÖBB offers direct connections to many European cities, including Bratislava, Budapest, Munich and Prague. For train information and bookings, visit oebb.at or call 05 17 17 (24 hours). Most trains arrive at and depart from one of two stations: Wien Hauptbahnhof

(Main Railway Station; Am Hauptbahnhof 1; U1 to Südtiroler Platz/Hauptbahnhof) or Wien Westbahnhof (Western Railway Station; Europaplatz 2; U3, U6 to Westbahnhof).

As a rule, most international trains, including from Prague, Bratislava and Budapest, use Wien Hauptbahnhof, while trains from Germany, western Europe and western Austria use Wien Westbahnhof. Be sure to check your ticket carefully to make certain which station your train is using.

ARRIVING BY CAR

Vienna is reached from Germany, Salzburg and Linz via the West Autobahn (A1); from the Italian and Slovenian borders and Graz it is reached via the South Autobahn (A2); from the Hungarian and Slovak borders it is reached via the East Autobahn (A4); and from the Czech border it is reached from Prague via the North Autobahn (A22) and from Brno via the future A5.

All motorists are obliged to purchase a wind-shield sticker—a *maut pickerl*—at the border, which serves as a general highway toll. A 10-day sticker costs €9. Tolls are also payable in most neighboring countries.

ARRIVING BY BUS

International bus lines (eurolines.at) arrive at the bus terminal at Erdbergstrasse 200A opposite U3 Erdberg (tel 798 29 00). The S-Bahn leaves from here, along with tram 18.

ARRIVING BY BOAT

From June to September, weekly cruise ships run on the Danube between Passau (Germany) and Vienna. From May to early October, there is a hydrofoil connection to Budapest three times a week (daily in August). Ships dock at the DDSG (ddsg-blue-danube.at) berth near the Reichsbrücke. From late March to mid-October the Twin City Liner hydrofoil (▷ 94) runs several times daily to Bratislava from the ferry station at Schwedenbrücke.

INSURANCE

EU nationals receive reduced-cost medical treatment with the EHIC (European Health Insurance Card)—obtain this before you go. Full health and travel insurance is still advised. US visitors should check their health cover before departure and buy a supplementary policy if necessary.

VISITORS WITH DISABILITIES

Facilities have improved in museums and some other major sights, but access is not always guaranteed. Older trams and buses remain impossible for anyone in a wheelchair, but most U-Bahn stations are now better equipped with escalators and elevators, and tram stops now indicate on their display boards whether the approaching trams have lowered platforms for alighting. The tourist board website (vienna.info) gives the detailed status of transportation, hotels, sights, museums and more. The tourist office also publishes a 130-page guide for visitors with disabilities. It is regularly updated, and can be downloaded from the same website.

Getting Around

TAXIS

● Cabs are efficient and not unreasonably expensive by Austrian standards.
● You can order a cab by phone: tel 31 300, 40 100 or 60 160.
● Tips are 10 percent.
● There are supplements for late-night or weekend rides, plus per head and per piece of luggage.
● Taxis ordered by telephone usually arrive in about five minutes in the heart of the city and inner suburbs.

Vienna is covered by an overlapping network of U-Bahnen (underground trains), Strassenbahnen (trams) and buses. Newsagents (*Tabaktrafik*) sell tickets for public transportation. Main U-Bahn and S-Bahn (rapid-transit railway) stations have ticket counters and all have ticket machines. Taxis can be hired at taxi stands in the city and at the larger public transportation terminals. Officially it is not permitted to hail them in the street, but some will stop for you.

INTEGRATED SYSTEM
● Maps and information about the transportation network can be obtained at the Wiener Linien information office at the Karlsplatz end of Opern Passage (tel 790 91 00) or on the website at wienerlinien.at.
● Buy tickets for the U-Bahn, Strassenbahn, buses or S-Bahn from newsagents or at the counters in main U-Bahn and S-Bahn stations. An easy one to find is at the Karlsplatz end of the Opern Passage, at the entrance to U1, U2, U4.
● A single journey card must be validated at the entrance to the underground, or on a tram or bus, using the stamping machines. It can be used for one unbroken ride, including changes of line, or changes from S-Bahn/U-Bahn to tram, to bus. It is valid one hour from stamping.
● Penalties for riding without a valid ticket are heavy and checks are quite frequent.

TYPES OF TICKET
● Excursion or season tickets are valid on all parts of the network and even on suburban buses (up to the city boundary).
● Individual tickets are much more expensive per ride, and the machines dispensing them on trams are complicated.
● Good-value monthly or weekly tickets allow unlimited travel all over the network for their duration. No photo is required.
● The *8 Tage-Karte* provides a book of eight strips, each valid for travel all over the network

the day it is validated until 1am the following day. If there are two or more of you, validate one strip per person. Start with strip No. 1.

● You can buy blocks of tickets for single rides, as well as 24-hour and 72-hour time tickets (useful for short-term visitors).

● Time tickets and the *8 Tage-Karte* must be validated at the commencement of the period of use and are then good for the period stipulated.

● *Wien-Karte* is a 48-hour or 72-hour card with discounts on entry charges to many sights.

● Children under six travel free.

U-BAHN

● There are five lines. Oddly, there is U1, U2, U3, U4 and U6 but no U5. U2 follows a semicircular route around the Ringstrasse and beyond.

● The U-Bahn maps found on platforms are color-coded and also show connections to other forms of transportation. Note the end-stop of the direction you want; this will be shown on the sign of the appropriate platform.

● Three lines (U1, U2, U4) meet at Karlsplatz/Oper.

● Main stations have lifts and/or escalators.

● You may take bicycles into designated cars on the U-Bahn (except during rush hour) for an additional charge.

● The S-Bahn (*Schnellbahn*) is a rapid-transit railway bringing commuters from the suburbs to the major traffic connections of the city.

TRAMS/BUSES

● The route is clearly marked at the tram stop and on a card inside. Check you are going in the right direction.

● Bus routes fill the gaps between the mostly radial tram lines. Night buses on main routes run every 30 minutes from Schwedenplatz after 12.30am until around 5am.

● The small hopper buses (1A, 2A and 3A) have circular routes through the Inner City with stops at or near virtually all places of interest.

SENSIBLE PRECAUTIONS

● Lock valuables in your hotel safe and don't carry large amounts of cash. Crime is low in Vienna, but in high-season pickpockets are busy.

● Avoid the main railway stations at night and the red-light district along the Gürtel.

DRIVING

● Avoid taking your car into the districts inside the Gürtel and especially into the old city inside the Ringstrasse, where underground parking is expensive and above-ground parking difficult and complicated.

CITY BIKE CARD

● At around 120 self-service stations you may rent a bike with a City Bike Card at a very low rate (visit citybikewien.at for details on how to obtain a card, but note you'll have to enter a valid credit or debit card number).

Essential Facts

- **Australia**
  ✉ Mattiellistrasse 2–4
  ☎ 506 740
- **Canada**
  ✉ Laurenzerberg 2
  ☎ 531 38 30 10
- **Ireland**
  ✉ Rotenturm-strasse 16–18 ☎ 715 42 46
- **New Zealand**
  ✉ Mattiellistrasse 2–4/3
  ☎ 505 30 21
- **UK**
  ✉ Jaurésgasse 12
  ☎ 71 61 30
- **US**
  ✉ Boltzmanngasse 16
  ☎ 313 390 (embassy) or
  ✉ Parkring 12A ☎ 31 339 75 35 (consulate)

MONEY

The euro (€) is Austria's official currency. Notes are in denominations of 5, 10, 20, 50, 100, 200 and 500 euros, and coins in 1 and 2 euros and 1, 2, 5, 10, 20 and 50 cents.

ELECTRICITY

- The voltage is 220 volts AC and two-pin plugs are used.

ETIQUETTE

- Titles are important; if you know which one to use (eg *Herr Doktor*), use it. Address the waiter as *Herr Ober*, the waitress as *Fräulein*.

LOST PROPERTY

- Report loss or theft to the nearest police station.
- Lost and Found Office at Bastiengasse 36–38 (tel 4000 8091, open Mon–Fri 8–3, Thu 8–5.30).
- Railway Lost Property (tel 930 00 22 222).
- Vienna Transport System Lost Property (tel 7909 43 188).

MEDICAL TREATMENT

- Vienna General Hospital (Allgemeines Krankenhaus) is at Währinger Gürtel 18–20 (tel 404 000, akhwien.at).
- The Barmherzige Brüder (Brothers of Mercy) treat patients free of charge at their hospital on Johannes von Gott Platz 1 (2nd District, tel 211 210, barmherzige-brueder.at).

MONEY MATTERS

- Credit cards are accepted by most hotels, leading shops and more expensive restaurants.
- Bankomat machines giving cash using international credit or debit cards with PIN numbers are plentiful in the city.

NATIONAL HOLIDAYS

- 1 Jan
- 6 Jan (Epiphany)
- Easter Monday
- 1 May (State Holiday)
- *Christi Himmelfahrt* (Ascension Day)
- Whit Monday
- Corpus Christi (second Thu after Whitsun)
- 15 Aug (Assumption of the Virgin)
- 26 Oct (National Day)

- 1 Nov (All Saints)
- 8 Dec (Conception)
- 24–26 Dec (everything closes from midday on Christmas Eve)

OPENING HOURS

- Shops: Mon–Fri 9–6, Sat 9–5 (food shops may open earlier). Retailers have a choice of whether to open on Saturdays, and many—particularly outside the center—prefer to stay closed or open only until noon. Most shops open 9–6 on the four Saturdays before Christmas.
- Banks: Mon–Fri 8–12.30, 1.30–3; Thu 1.30–5.30. In the city some stay open at lunch.
- Offices: Mon–Fri 8–4, but may close earlier on Friday.

PHARMACIES

- Pharmacies normally open Mon–Fri 8–12, 2–6, Sat 8–12.
- English-speaking pharmacists include Internationale Apotheke (Kärntner Ring 17, tel 512 28 25), Schweden-Apotheke, Pharmacie Internationale (Schwedenplatz 2, tel 533 2911).

POST OFFICES

- There is a general website for the postal system at post.at.
- Fleischmarkt 19, tel 0577 677 10 10, open Mon–Fri 7am–10pm, Sat–Sun 9am–10pm.
- Westbahnhof, tel 832 61 10, open Mon–Fri 7am–9pm, Sat 9–6, Sun 9–2.

TELEPHONES

- Telephone cards are sold in *Tabaktrafik* shops (newsagents) and at post offices. Some telephones in the Kohlmarkt/Graben area take credit cards.
- To call Vienna from the UK dial 00431. To call the UK from Vienna, dial 0044.
- To call Vienna from the US dial 011431. To call the US from Vienna, dial 001.
- Directory assistance for Austria and the EU is on 118 877; for everywhere else call 0900 11 8877.

TOURIST INFORMATION

- Tourist-Info Wien ☎ 24 555, vienna.info
- **Main Branch**
  ✉ Albertinaplatz (corner of Maysedergasse)
  🕐 Daily 9–7
- **Vienna International Airport**
  ✉ Arrivals Hall 🕐 Daily 7am–10pm
- **Main Train Station**
  ✉ Am Hauptbahnhof 1
  🕐 Daily 9–7

Language

The Austrian variant of *Hochdeutsch* (High German) is marked enough to warrant a small dictionary for German visitors, but will not trouble the foreign tourist who has learned German. *Wienerisch* (the local dialect of the Viennese) is more difficult, but most natives will respond with the *Hochdeutsch* they have learned in school if addressed in this way by a foreigner.

THE BASICS

ja	yes
nein	no
bitte	please
danke	thank you
bitte schön	you're welcome
Grüss Gott	hello
guten Morgen	good morning
guten Abend	good evening
gute Nacht	good night
auf Wiedersehen	goodbye
Entschuldigen Sie bitte	Excuse me please
Sprechen Sie Englisch?	Do you speak English?
ich verstehe nicht	I don't understand
Wiederholen Sie das, bitte	Please repeat that
Sprechen Sie langsamer bitte	Please speak more slowly
heute	today
gestern	yesterday
morgen	tomorrow
jetzt	now
gut	good
Ich heisse...	My name is...
Wie heissen Sie?	What's your name?
Ich komme aus...	I'm from...
Wie geht es Ihnen?	How are you?
Sehr gut, danke	Fine, thank you
Wie spät ist es?	What is the time?
wo	where
wann	when
warum	why
wer	who

USEFUL WORDS

klein/gross	small/large
kalt/warm	cold/warm
rechts/links	right/left
geradeaus	straight ahead
nahe/weit	near/far
geschlossen	closed
offen	open

OUT AND ABOUT	
Wieviel kostet es?	How much does it cost?
teuer	expensive
billig	inexpensive
Wo sind die Toiletten?	Where are the toilets?
Wo ist die Bank?	Where's the bank?
der Bahnhof	station
der Flughafen	airport
das Postamt	post office
die Apotheke	pharmacy
die Polizei	police
das Krankenhaus	hospital
der Arzt	doctor
Hilfe	help
Haben Sie einen Stadtplan?	Do you have a city map?
Fahren Sie mich bitte zum/zur/nach...	Please take me to...
Ich möchte hier aussteigen	I'd like to get out here
Ich habe mich verlaufen/ verfahren	I am lost
Können Sie mir helfen?	Can you help me?

NUMBERS	
eins	1
zwei	2
drei	3
vier	4
fünf	5
sechs	6
sieben	7
acht	8
neun	9
zehn	10
elf	11
zwölf	12
dreizehn	13
zwanzig	20
einundzwanzig	21
dreissig	30
vierzig	40
fünfzig	50
sechzig	60
siebzig	70
achtzig	80
neunzig	90
hundert	100
tausend	1000
million	million

AT THE HOTEL/RESTAURANT	
die Speisekarte	menu
das Frühstück	breakfast
das Mittagesen	lunch
das Abendessen	dinner
der Weisswein	white wine
der Rotwein	red wine
das Bier	beer
das Brot	bread
die Milch	milk
der Zucker	sugar
das Wasser	water
die Rechnung	bill (check)
das Zimmer	room
Ich bin allergisch gegen...	I am allergic to...
Ich bin Vegetarier	I am a vegetarian

COLORS	
schwarz	black
blau	blue
braun	brown
rot	red
grün	green
weiss	white
gelb	yellow
rosa	pink
orange	orange
grau	grey
lila	purple

Timeline

Music has reverberated around Vienna since the days when the *Minnesänger* (poets of chivalry) performed at the Babenberg court in the 13th century. Members of the Habsburg dynasty were patrons of Gluck, Haydn, Mozart and Beethoven, among others.

Key musical dates include:

1782 Mozart's opera *The Abduction from the Seraglio* premieres at the Court Theater.

1792 Beethoven settles in Vienna.

1828 In June, Franz Schubert completes *Die Winterreise* song cycle. He dies 19 November, age 31.

1867 Johann Strauss Junior's *On the Beautiful Blue Danube* is performed by the Vienna Male Choral Society; it flops.

1897 Gustav Mahler becomes director of the Vienna opera, initiating a period of imaginative productions.

5th–1st century BC The Celtic Boier tribe settles on the site of today's Belvedere Palace.

15BC The Romans conquer the area. The city they establish on the Danube is called Vindobona.

AD400–791 The Romans withdraw. Charlemagne creates the *Ostmark* (Eastern Region of his empire).

881 The Salzburg annals recall a battle at *Weniam*—the first reference to the name *Wien* (Vienna).

1156 Austria becomes a Babenberg dukedom and Vienna the ducal residence.

1278 640 years of Habsburg rule begins.

1421 Savage violence against the Viennese Jews. Two hundred are burned alive.

1517 The advent of Lutheranism in Vienna.

1521 The Spanish and German realms of the Habsburgs, ruled by Charles V, are divided. Charles's brother, Ferdinand I, takes Austria.

1529 The first Turkish siege of Vienna.

1551 The Jesuits are invited to the city. The Counter-Reformation begins.

1683 The second Turkish siege attempt.

1805–15 Napoleon's troops twice occupy Vienna. After his defeat, the Congress of Vienna imposes order on Europe.

1848 Eighteen-year-old Franz Joseph becomes emperor.

1867 Austro-Hungarian Monarchy created.

1916 Franz Joseph dies. The Habsburg Empire is dissolved in 1918.

1922 Vienna becomes one of the Federal States of the Republic of Austria.

1934 Civil War breaks out. Clerico-Fascist dictatorship under Engelbert Dollfuss follows.

1938 Hitler annexes Austria.

1945–55 Vienna is under joint Allied control until the State Treaty restores a free Austrian state.

1995 Austria joins the European Union.

2017 Sebastian Kurz becomes Austrian Chancellor, ushering in a period of right-wing populism in Austria.

2022 The next Austrian legislative election will be on or before 6 November 2022.

THE RINGSTRASSE

On Christmas Day 1857 Emperor Franz Joseph ordered the demolition of the city bastions and the creation of a great boulevard around the city. The Ringstrasse symbolized an era of wealth, industry and modernization.

THE *ANSCHLUSS*

After the *Anschluss*—the annexation of Austria to Germany by Adolf Hitler— many Viennese went into exile, and artistic and academic talent was lost through Austrian-born Adolf Eichmann's campaign to make Vienna *judenrein* (Jew-free).

Habsburg crown; double-headed eagle; Strauss Monument; Secession's dome of gilded laurel leaves (left to right)

Index

A

Academy of Fine Arts 8, 50, 59
accommodations 17, 18, 107–112
air travel 116
Akademie der Bildenden Künste
   8, 50, 59
Albertina 32, 36
Alsergrund 65–76
   entertainment and nightlife 74
   map 66–67
   shopping 73
   sights 68–71
   walk 72
   where to eat 75–76
Altes Rathaus 28
amusement park 8, 98
Ankeruhr 17, 28
Annakirche 32, 36
antiques and art 12, 16, 38, 39, 40
Architekturzentrum 54
Arsenal and Museum of Military
   History 9, 80
Artaria Haus 32
Augarten 100
Augarten Contemporary 100
Augustinerkirche 32, 36
Austrian Film Museum 41
Austrian Post Office Savings Bank
   18, 34, 59
Austrian Theatre Museum 34

B

Baden 102
bankomat machines 120
banks 121
Belvedere Palace 7, 8, 82–83, 86
Bestattungsmuseum 100
bike hire 119
bookshops 12, 38–39, 40, 60
Bratislava 94, 102
Burggarten 32
Burgtheater 8, 51, 59, 61
Burial Museum 100
buses
   city 119
   long-distance 117

C

Capuchin Crypt 6, 9, 29
Carriage Museum 99
children 18
Children's Museum 54
Christkindlmarkt 60
churches
   Annakirche 32, 36
   Augustinerkirche 32, 36
   Jesuitenkirche 34
   Kaisergruft 6, 9, 29
   Karlskirche 9, 81, 86
   Kirche am Steinhof 18, 100
   Peterskirche 35, 36
   Schottenkirche 25
   Servitenkirche 71, 72
   Stephansdom 6, 8, 17, 31, 36
   Votivkirche 59, 71, 72
   Wotruba Kirche 101

City Hall see Altes Rathaus;
   Rathaus
climate and seasons 114
Clock Museum 35
clubs see entertainment
   and nightlife
coffeehouses 8, 15, 16, 24, 43,
   44, 62, 75
credit cards 120
crime 119
cruise ships 94, 117
customs regulations 116

D

Danube Cruise 9, 94
Danube National Park 94
disabilities, visitors with 117
Donauinsel 94
Donner Brunnen 33
dress, traditional 10, 73, 87
driving 117, 119
Dürnstein 104

E

eating out 5, 14–15, 17, 18
   Viennese cuisine 14, 15, 63
   see also where to eat
electricity 120
embassies and consulates 120
emergency telephone numbers
   121
entertainment and nightlife 13, 17
   Alsergrund 74
   Farther Afield 105
   Innere Stadt 41–42
   Landstrasse, Wieden 88
   Ringstrasse 61
Esperanto Museum 33
etiquette 120
excursions 102–104

F

Farther Afield 91–106
   entertainment and nightlife
      105
   excursions 102–104
   map 92–93
   shopping 105
   sights 94–101
   where to eat 106
Ferris wheel 8, 18, 98
festivals and events 4, 114
food and drink
   Sachertorte 6, 10, 16, 39
   shopping for 10–11, 12, 38, 39,
      40, 60, 73, 87
   see also eating out
Freud Haus 9, 68–69, 72
Freyung 9, 25, 36

G

Gänsehäufel 100
gifts and souvenirs 10
glass and porcelain 10, 12, 16, 38,
   39, 40, 60, 105
Globenmuseum 33

H

Haus der Musik 16, 33
Haus des Meeres 57
Heeresgeschichtliches Museum
   9, 80, 86
Heiligenkreuz 102
Heiligenstadt 96
Heurigen 13, 14, 15, 96, 106
history 124–125
Hitler, Adolf 50, 125
Hochstrahlbrunnen 7, 85, 86
Hofburg 4, 6, 9, 26–27, 36
Hofmobiliendepot 57
Hohe Warte Secessionist
   Villa Colony 96
Hoher Markt 28
Holocaust Memorial 28
hotels 17, 18, 108, 109–112
Hundertwasser-Haus 9, 95

I

Imperial Treasury 26, 27, 36
Innere Stadt 20–46
   entertainment and nightlife
      41–42
   map 22–23
   shopping 38–40
   sights 24–35
   walk 36–37
   where to eat 43–46
insurance 117

J

Jesuitenkirche 34
Jewish Museum 28
Jewish Quarter 7, 9, 28
Josephinum 71, 72
Jugendstil 30, 32, 40, 56, 57, 88

K

Kahlenburg 9, 96
Kaiserin Elisabeth Denkmal 57
Kaisergruft 6, 9, 29
Karl-Marx-Hof 96
Karlskirche 9, 81, 86
Kinsky-Palais 25
Kirche am Steinhof 18, 100
Klimt, Gustav 8, 18, 51, 54,
   56, 83
Klosterneuburg 103
KunstHausWien 9, 95
Kunsthistorisches Museum
   6, 9, 52–53

L

Landstrasse, Wieden 77–90
   entertainment and nightlife
      88
   map 78–79
   shopping 87
   sights 80–85
   walk 86
   where to eat 89–90
language 4, 122–123
Laxenburg 103
Leopold Museum 54

Lobkowitz-Palais 34
lost property 120

M
markets 12, 60
medical treatment 117, 120, 121
Melk 104
money 120
Mozarthaus 6, 16, 34
museums and galleries
    Akademie der Bildenden Künste
        8, 50
    Albertina 32, 36
    Arsenal and Museum of Military
        History 9, 80
    Augarten Contemporary 100
    Austrian Film Museum 41
    Austrian Theatre Museum 34
    Bestattungsmuseum 100
    Burial Museum 100
    Carriage Museum 99
    Children's Museum 54
    Clock Museum 35
    Esperanto Museum 33
    Freud Haus 9, 68–69, 72
    Globenmuseum 33
    Haus der Musik 16, 33
    Heeresgeschichtliches Museum
        9, 80, 86
    Jewish Museum 28
    Kunsthistorisches Museum 6, 9,
        52–53, 59
    Leopold Museum 54
    Museum of Applied Art 9,
        30, 59
    Museum of Art History
        9, 52–53, 59
    Museum für Angewandte Kunst
        (MAK) 9, 30, 59
    Museum of Medical History
        71, 72
    Museum of Modern Art 54
    Museum for Pathology
        and Anatomy 98
    Narrenturm 71, 72
    Natural History Museum
        52, 53, 58, 59
    Naturhistorisches Museum 52,
        53, 58, 59
    Palais Liechtenstein 8, 70, 72
    Schloss Belvedere 8, 82–83, 86
    Sisi Museum 27
    Technisches Museum 100–101
    Tramway Museum 101
    Uhrenmuseum 35
    Wien Museum 8, 84
    Wiener Strassenbahnmuseum
        101
MuseumsQuartier 9, 54
music 114, 124
    classical 11, 16, 42, 74, 88, 97
    concert venues 61, 88, 97
    jazz 41, 42
    opera 35, 42, 74, 105
Musikverein 7, 16, 88
MuTh 8, 97

N
Narrenturm 71, 72
Naschmarkt 57
national holidays 120–121
National Library 27, 36
Nationalbibliothek 26, 27, 36
Natural History Museum
    52, 53, 58, 59
Naturhistorisches Museum
    52, 53, 58, 59

O
office hours 121
opening hours 121
Österreichisches Postparkassenamt
    18, 34, 59
Österreichisches Filmmuseum 41
Otto Wagner Pavillon 35

P
Palais Ferstel 25
Palais Liechtenstein 8, 70, 72
Palais-Schwarzenberg 85
Parlament 58, 59
passports 116
Peterskirche 35, 36
pharmacies 121
police 121
population 4
post offices 121
Prater 7, 8, 18, 98
private room accommodations
    109
public transportation 118–119

R
Rathaus 8, 55, 59
Rathausplatz 4
    Alsergrund 75–76
    Farther Afield 106
    Innere Stadt 43–46
    Landstrasse, Wieden 89–90
    Ringstrasse 62–64
Riesenrad 8, 98
Ringstrasse 47–64, 125
    entertainment and nightlife 61
    map 48–49
    shopping 60
    sights 50–58
    walk 59
    where to eat 62–64
Russian Liberation Monument
    85, 86

S
St. Charles's Church 9, 81
St. Stephen's Cathedral 6, 8, 17,
    31, 36
Schatzkammer 26, 27, 36
Schloss Belvedere 7, 8, 82–83
Schloss Schönbrunn 8, 18, 99
Schottenkirche 25
Schubert, Franz 74
Secession 8, 18, 56
security 119
Seegrotte Hinterbrühl 18, 104

Semmering 104
Servitenkirche 71, 72
shopping 10–12, 16
    Alsergrund 73
    Farther Afield 105
    Innere Stadt 38–40
    Landstrasse, Wieden 87
    Ringstrasse 60
Sisi Museum 27
Spanish Riding School 4, 26–27
Spittelberg 13, 60
Staatsoper 7, 35, 36, 42, 59
Stadtpark 35, 59
Stadttempel 28
State Opera 7, 35, 36, 42, 59
Steinhof Church 18, 100
Stephansdom 6, 8, 17, 31, 36
Strauss Denkmal 35, 59
Strudlhofstiege 71, 72

T
Tanzquartier 54
taxis 118
Technisches Museum 100–101
telephones 121
Theater an der Wien 58, 61
theater 41, 51, 58, 59, 61, 74, 97
time differences 114
tipping 118
tourist information 115, 121
trains 116–117
trams 119
Tramway Museum 101
Twin City Liner 94, 117
two-day itinerary 6–7

U
U-Bahn 118, 119
Uhrenmuseum 35

V
vaccinations 116
Vienna Boys' Choir 4, 26, 97, 100
Viennese Transport Museum 8, 84
Volksgarten 58, 59
Votivkirche 59, 71, 72

W
Wachau Valley 104
walks
    Alsergrund Stroll 72
    Baroque at its Best 86
    Old Vienna 36
    Ringstrasse Circle 59
websites 115
where to eat 15, 17
Wien Museum 8, 84
Wiener Strassenbahnmuseum 101
wine taverns 13, 14, 15, 96, 106
Wittgenstein Haus 101
Wotruba Kirche 101

Z
zoo 99

CityPack Vienna

Published by AA Publishing, a trading name of AA Media Limited, whose registered office is Fanum House, Basing View, Basingstoke, Hampshire RG21 4EA. Registered number 06112600.

© AA Media Limited 2019
First published 1996
New edition 2019

Written by Louis James
Updated by Marc di Duca
Series editor Clare Ashton
Design work Liz Baldin
Colour reprographics Ian Little

Printed and bound in China by 1010 Printing Group Limited

A CIP catalogue record for this book is available from the British Library.

ISBN 978-0-7495-8181-7

A05671
Maps in this title produced from mapping data supplied by Global Mapping, Brackley, UK © Global Mapping and data available from openstreetmap.org © under the Open Database License found at opendatacommons.org
Transport map © Communicarta Ltd, UK

We would like to thank the following photographers, companies and picture libraries for their assistance in the preparation of this book.

2-18t © Österreich Werbung/Wiesenhofer; 4tl AA/J Smith; 5 AA/J Smith; 6cl © Österreich Werbung/Markowitsch; 6c © Österreich Werbung/Trumler; 6cr AA/J Smith; 6bl © Österreich Werbung/Bartl; 6bc AA/Clive Sawyer; 6br David Noble; 7cl © Österreich Werbung/Bartl; 7c AA/J Smith; 7cr © Österreich Werbung/Bartl; 7bl AA/J Smith; 7bc AA/Terry Harris; 7br © Österreich Werbung/Bartl; 10/11tc © Österreich Werbung/Bartl; 10c © Österreich Werbung/Bartl; 10/11bc AA/J Smith; 10/11b © Österreich Werbung/Kalmar; 11c © Österreich Werbung/Bartl; 13tl AA/David Noble; 13c B.O'Kane/Alamy; 13b © Österreich Werbung/Kalmar; 14tr AA/J Smith; 14tcr AA/J Smith; 14cbr AA/J Smith; 14br AA/David Noble; 16tr © Österreich Werbung/Trumler; 16tcr © Österreich Werbung/Kalmar; 16bcr AA/M Siebert; 16br Szaszi Hüte; 17tl AA/J Smith; 17tcl © Österreich Werbung/Kalmar; 17bcl © Österreich Werbung/Bartl; 17bl © Österreich Werbung/Popp G.; 18tr AA/J Smith; 18tcr © Österreich Werbung/Markowitsch; 18bcr Time Out Hotel; 18br Stockbyte Royalty Free; 19© Österreich Werbung/Lammerhuber; 20 AA/J Smith; 24tl F1online digitale Bildagentur GmbH/Alamy; 24tr imageBROKER/Alamy; 25tl © Österreich Werbung/Diejun; 25tc AA/J Smith; 25tr AA/J Smith; 26l AA/Clive Sawyer; 26/7t Copyright Schloss Schönbrunn Kultur- und Betriebsges.m.b.H./A E Koller ; 26/7c Copyright Schloss Schönbrunn Kultur- und Betriebsges.m.b.H./Lois Lammerhuber ; 27t Copyright Schloss Schönbrunn Kultur- und Betriebsges.m.b.H./A E Koller ; 27cr Copyright Schloss Schönbrunn Kultur- und Betriebsges.m.b.H./Wagner; 28tl AA/J Smith; 28tr AA/J Smith; 29tl © Österreich Werbung/Muhr; 29tr © Österreich Werbung/Muhr; 30tl © Österreich Werbung/Trumler ; 30tc © MAK/Katrin Wißkirchen; 30tr © Österreich Werbung/Trumler; 31tl AA/J Smith; 31tr AA/J Smith; 32-35t AA/J Smith; 32bl AA/J Smith; 33bl Haus der Musik; 33br © Austrian National Library; 34bl AA/David Noble; 34br Mozarthaus, Vienna; 35b AA/J Smith; 36t AA/J Smith; 37 © MAK/Katrin Wißkirchen; 38-40t © Österreich Werbung/H. Wiesenhofer; 41-42t © Österreich Werbung/Wiesenhofer; 43-45t AA/Clive Sawyer; 46 © Österreich Werbung/Bartl; 47 © Österreich Werbung/Haase; 50tl © Österreich Werbung/Kalmar; 50tc AA/J Smith; 50tr AA/J Smith; 51tl © Georg Soulek/Burgtheater; 51tr © Georg Soulek/Burgtheater; 52l AA/J Smith; 52tr © Österreich Werbung/Trumler; 52c © Österreich Werbung/Kalmar; 53 © Österreich Werbung/Bohnacker; 54 MuseumsQuartier © Alexander Eugen Koller; 55tl AA/David Noble; 55tr AA/J Smith; 56tl AA/J Smith; 56tr AA/J Smith; 57-58t AA/J Smith; 57bl Haus des Meeres; 57br © Bmobv, Lois Lammerhuber; 58br AA/J Smith; 58bl Naturhistorisches Museum/Alice Schumacher; 59t AA/J Smith; 60t © Österreich Werbung/H.Wiesenhofer; 61t © Österreich Werbung/Wiesenhofer; 62-63t AA/Clive Sawyer; 64 Leopold Museum, Wien; 65 AA/J Smith; 68l AA/J Smith; 68/69 AA/J Smith; 69t © Österreich Werbung/Kalmar; 69b Gaia Vittoria Marturano/Alamy; 70tl AA/J Smith; 70tr © Österreich Werbung/Diejun; 71t A/J Smith; 71bl AA/M Siebert; 72t AA/J Smith; 73t © Österreich Werbung/H.Wiesenhofer; 74t © Österreich Werbung/Wiesenhofer; 75t AA/Clive Sawyer; 76 Simon Reddy/Alamy; 77 AA/J Smith; 80tl AA/J Smith; 80tr AA/J Smith; 81tl AA/Michael Siebert; 81tc AA/J Smith; 81tr Verein Karlskirche; 82–83 © Belvedere, Vienna; 84tl AA/J Smith; 84tr AA/J Smith; 85t AA/J Smith; 85b manfredrf/ Alamy; 86t AA/J Smith; 87t © Österreich Werbung/H.Wiesenhofer; 88t © Österreich Werbung/Wiesenhofer; 89t AA/Clive Sawyer; 90 CuboImages srl/Alamy; 91 © Österreich Werbung/Hedgecoe (London); 94tl John Peter Photography/Alamy; 94tr Viennaslide/Alamy; 95tl © Österreich Werbung/H.Wiesenhofer; 95tr © Österreich Werbung/Wiesenhofer; 96t AA/J Smith; 97t Grethe Ulgjell/Alamy; 98tl © Prater, Wien; 98tr Michael Siebert; 99t Copyright Schloss Schönbrunn Kultur- und Betriebsges.m.b.H./Alexander Eugen Koller; 100b AA/J Smith; 101b © Österreich Werbung/Wiesenhofer; 102-104t © Österreich Werbung/Diejun; 105t © Österreich Werbung/H.Wiesenhofer; 105c © Österreich Werbung/Wiesenhofer; 106t AA/Clive Sawyer; 108-112t AA/Clive Sawyer; 108tr AA/J Smith; 108tcr dpa picture alliance/Alamy; 108cr © Österreich Werbung/Kalmar; 108br © Österreich Werbung/Kalmar; 114-125t AA/J Smith; 122br AA/J Smith; 124bl © Österreich Werbung/Wiesenhofer; 124br © Österreich Werbung/Wiesenhofer; 125bl AA/J Smith; 125br AA/J Smith.

Every effort has been made to trace the copyright holders, and we apologise in advance for any unintentional omissions or errors. We would be pleased to apply any corrections in a following edition of this publication.

Titles in the Series

- Amsterdam
- Bangkok
- Barcelona
- Berlin
- Boston
- Brussels & Bruges
- Budapest
- Dubai
- Dublin
- Edinburgh
- Florence
- Hong Kong
- Istanbul
- Krakow
- Las Vegas
- Lisbon
- London
- Madrid
- Milan
- Munich
- New York
- Orlando
- Paris
- Prague
- Rome
- San Francisco
- Shanghai
- Singapore
- Sydney
- Toronto
- Venice
- Vienna
- Washington